0-07-044129-4	H. MURPHY	Assembler for COBOL Programmers: MVS, VM
0-07-006533-0	H. BOOKMAN	COBOL II
0-07-051244-2	J. RANADE	VSAM: Concepts, Programming and Design
0-07-051245-0	J. RANADE	VSAM: Performance, Design and Fine Tuning
0-07-051143-8	J. RANADE	Advanced SNA Networking: A Professional's Guide for Using VTAM/NCP
0-07-051144-6	J. RANADE	Introduction to SNA Networking: A Guide to VTAM/NCP
0-07-051264-7	J. RANADE	DOS to OS/2: Conversion, Migration, and Application Design
0-07-051265-5	J. RANADE	DB2: Concepts, Programming and Design
0-07-054594-4	J. SANCHEZ	IBM Microcomputers Handbook
0-07-054597-9	J. SANCHEZ	Programming Solutions Handbook for IBM Microcomputers
0-07-009816-6	M. CARATHANASSIS	Expert MVS/XA JCL: A Complete Guide to Advanced Techniques
0-07-009820-4	M. CARATHANASSIS	Expert MVS/ESA JCL: A Guide to Advanced Techniques
0-07-017606-X	P. DONOFRIO	CICS: Debugging, Dump Reading and Problem Determination
0-07-017607-8	P. DONOFRIO	CICS: A Programmer's Reference
0-07-018966-8	T. EDDOLLS	VM Performance Management
0-07-033571-0	P. KAVANAGH	VS COBOL II for COBOL Programmers
0-07-040666-9	T. MARTYN	DB2/SQL: A Professional Programmer's Guide
0-07-050054-1	S. PIGGOT	CICS: A Practical Guide to System Fine Tuning
0-07-050686-8	N. PRASAD	IBM Mainframes: Architecture and Design
0-07-054528-6	S. SAMSON	MVS Performance Management
0-07-032673-8	B. JOHNSON	MVS: Concepts and Facilities
0-07-032674-6	B. JOHNSON, D. JOHNSON	DASD: IBM's Direct Access Storage Devices
0-07-071136-4	A. WIPFLER	Distributed Processing in the CICS Environment
0-07-071139-9	A. WIPFLER	CICS Application Development Programming
0-07-007252-3	K. BRATHWAITE	Relational Data Bases: Concepts, Design, and Administration
0-07-028682-8	G. GOLDBERG, P. SMITH	The REXX Handbook
0-07-040763-0	M. MARX, P. DAVIS	MVS Power Programming
0-07-057553-3	D. SILVERBERG	DB2: Performance, Design, and Implementation
0-07-069460-5	A. WERMAN	DB2 Handbook for DBAs
0-07-002553-3	G. HOUTEKAMER, P. ARTIS	MVS I/O Subsystem: Configuration Management and Performance Analysis
0-07-033727-6	A. KAPOOR	SNA: Architecture, Protocols, and Implementation
0-07-014770-1	R. CROWNHART	IBM's Workstation CICS
0-07-015305-1	C. DANEY	Programming in REXX
0-07-037040-0	J. KNEILING, R. LEFKON, P. SOMERS	Understanding CICS Internals
0-07-022453-6	A. FRIEND	Cobol Application Debugging Under MVS: Cobol and Cobol II
0-07-008606-0	L. BRUMBAUGH	VSAM: Architecture, Theory, and Applications
0-07-040775-4	T. HARTLEY	Oracle/SQC: A Professional Programmer's Guide
0-07-054529-4	S. SAMSON	MVS Performance Management (ESA/390 edition)
0-07-018301-5	T. BARITZ	AS/400 Concepts and Facilities
0-07-039825-9	S. MALIK	CSP: A Developer's Guide

REXX

Advanced Techniques for Programmers

Peter C. Kiesel
Customer Education
IBM Corporation

McGraw-Hill, Inc.
New York St. Louis San Francisco Auckland Bogotá
Caracas Lisbon London Madrid Mexico Milan
Montreal New Delhi Paris San Juan São Paulo
Singapore Sydney Tokyo Toronto

This book is dedicated to my parents—Margaret and Conrad, without whose "guidance" I would have been a music major, and to my sisters—Mimi, Kathy, Mary Beth, Molly, and Peggy—because if I didn't mention them in this dedication I'd never hear the end of it.

Library of Congress Cataloging-in-Publication Data

Kiesel, Peter C.
    REXX : advanced techniques for programmers / Peter C. Kiesel.
       p.   cm.—(J. Ranade IBM series)
    Includes index.
    ISBN 0-07-034600-3
    1. REXX (Computer program language). I. Title. II. Series.
  QA76.73.R24K53 1993
    005.13'3—dc20   92-22231
                                        CIP

1 2 3 4 5 6 7 8 9 0 DOC/DOC 9 8 7 6 5 4 3 2

ISBN 0-07-034600-3

1659/21   *11-16-93*

The sponsoring editor for this book was Jerry Papke, the editing supervisor was Kimberly A. Goff, and the production supervisor was Pamela A. Pelton.

Printed and bound by R. R. Donnelley & Sons Company.

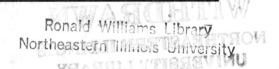

Contents

Figures

Preface

The REXX programming language has been available for some years now. Its spread in use is an indication of its popularity. It is a very easy language to learn, and it is very powerful. As with any other programming language or command processing language, there is a learning curve that one must encounter. Although learning curves are unique and the amount of time spent in each stage of the learning curve varies (based on the individual's skills and abilities), there are, nonetheless, many stages that are commonly encountered by all when learning REXX.

Over the past eight years, I have taught REXX to IBM's customers as well as IBM's employees. In addition, I have worked with REXX in a program development environment, both from a development and from a test angle. Many people have asked similar questions when learning the REXX language. This book is a compilation of the issues, questions, and concerns that people have had when working with the REXX language. Questions that address many different aspects of the REXX language are covered, for example:

- How is a subroutine different from a function in REXX?
- Does REXX have a GOTO statement?
- How do quotes work in REXX?
- Can I write a REXX program for my editor environment?
- How do I issue a host command from within REXX?
- Can you show me an example of how I can handle user input?
- How do I read/write files from REXX?
- etc.

This book has been written for the person who is learning the REXX language, as well as for the person who is somewhat experienced with the REXX language, but has some lingering questions. As you read this book, you will note that it seems different from most books in that it tries to explain the "why" of REXX, not just the "what" or "how."

Peter C. Kiesel

Part 1.
Coding
Techniques

Chapter 1.
Overall Format of Your Program

One of the "beauties" of REXX lies in its flexibility regarding program format. Each person writing a REXX program is allowed to use his/her own style; you might prefer to use all upper case letters when coding your program, and another person may prefer to use mixed case. You might prefer to write your program statements all on one line (don't forget the semicolons!), and another person may prefer to write program statements in a more vertical fashion. You may prefer to use 'A''s' to end up with A's, and another person may prefer to use "A's" to end up with A's. REXX allows you to make the decision regarding program format.

We will begin by looking at some of the aspects of program format, in particular:

Line continuation   Case (MiXeD/UPPER/lower)

Quotes   Indentation

Semicolons   Commenting

Several examples will be shown to demonstrate the different ways of coding REXX programs as they pertain to each of the above aspects. For those who are reading this book with the idea in mind "I wish someone would suggest a particular coding scheme," you're in luck. At the end of each aspect, there will be a suggested method. Since there are so many different ways to write REXX code, this is by no means the only correct way; instead, it is offered for those who are having difficulty deciding which way to code REXX statements. These suggestions, when "put together," will form a framework from which all REXX programs can be written.

Without further ado, let's go. Our first look will be at the idea of Line Continuation...

1.1   Line Continuation in REXX

Line continuation is used for the benefit of the program writer/reader, as opposed to the benefit of the interpreter. When writing your REXX program, you may need have a string that is rather long, and would not appear on the screen or the printout in a very readable format. This string may be part of any of the following:

IF statement

```
if filename = 'SAMPLE12' &,
   filetype = 'EXEC'     &,
   filemode = default_filemode &,
   go_ahead_flag = 'YES'
   then
   address command 'EXECIO 1 'filename filetype filemode '1 (FINIS ',
                   'LOCATE /'search_string'/ ZONE 10 20'
```

host command

```
address command 'EXECIO 1 'filename filetype filemode '1 (FINIS ',
                'STRING This is the first day of the rest of your life'
```

arithmetic expression

```
answer=input_amount*scaling_factor - (margin_allowance/margin_scale),
       +max(extra_input, 0)
```

---

variable assignment

```
phrases='Uh oh, this is starting to get kind of warm...',
        'remember the "eclipse"...what'"'s for dinner?"
```

SAY statement

```
say    "Uh oh, this is starting to get kind of warm...",
       "remember the 'eclipse'...what's for dinner?"
```

---

or part of some other REXX statement.

In order to "break" the statement (portion) physically, but not logically, line continuation is used to extend a clause across the physical end-of-line in a REXX exec. The comma (,) is recognized by the REXX interpreter as the line continuation character if it is the last character on a line (REXX will ignore in-line comments— see Figs. 1 and 2 on the next page). When the interpreter "joins" the clauses together, a blank space will be inserted in place of the comma.

The majority of the problems encountered with line continuation center around the use of line continuation with quoted strings. The string to be continued should be separated into two smaller strings, which allows the first string to be closed by a quote, and *then* use the comma. This is extremely important if there is an in-line comment; if the first string is not closed by a quote, the interpreter will search until it finds another quote (quotes must be used in pairs), and any in-line comments will become part of the quoted string (see Fig. 3). This will probably produce unwanted results at a later point in your exec.

Note: REXX will allow you to continue strings without using a continuation character (see Figs. 4 and 5). This method is not recommended; it is far too easy for someone who is maintaining the exec to place an in-line comment on the line containing the SAY instruction, which will then resemble Fig. 3.

1.1.1 Examples

Here are some examples of line continuation, along with their output:

```
/* example a */
say 'example_a:'
say 'this is string 1', /*this is in-line comment 1*/
'and continuation 1'

produces the following output:

this is string 1 and continuation 1
```

Figure 1. Valid use of line continuation.

Figure 1 shows the proper use of line continuation. In this case, a rather long character string is to be displayed on the screen. Keeping in mind that one blank will be substituted for the continuation character once the strings are concatenated, a "logical" break point in the output is used. The second string is then moved to the next physical line. The in-line comment is ignored.

```
/* example b */
say 'example_b:'
say 'this is string 2'  /*this is in-line comment 2*/,
'and continuation 2'

produces:

this is string 2 and continuation 2
```

Figure 2. Valid (but dangerous) use of line continuation.

Figure 2 shows a valid use of line continuation, but it leaves a
point of vulnerability, which could backfire on you at a later point
in time. The in-line comment is ignored, but the comma is at the
physical end of the line, and may be overlooked. If at some later
point a blank line (or perhaps another comment line) were to be
inserted between the SAY statement and the continuation line, the
continuation would never be picked up. Line continuation is
implied for the next line only. Additional line continuation
characters can/should be used to continue across more than one
line.

```
/* example c */
say 'example_c:'
say 'this is string 3    /*this is in-line comment 3*/
and continuation 3'

produces:

this is string 3   /*this is in-line comment 3*/and continuation 3
```

Figure 3. Invalid use of line continuation.

The error in Fig. 3 lies in not breaking the larger string into
two smaller strings and using the line continuation character to
tell REXX the rest of this is found on the next line. What this
statement is telling REXX is:

> Immediately following the Say is the beginning quote for
> this character string. Keep looking until you find the
> closing quote (even if it means looking across the end of a
> line).

REXX will keep looking and concatenating until it has amassed a
string of 500 characters. If the closing quote has not been found
by then, a syntax error occurs.

```
/* example d */
say 'example_d:'
say 'this is string 4,
and continuation 4'
```

produces:

this is string 4,and continuation 4

Figure 4. Invalid use of line continuation.

Figure 4 shows another possible consequence of not breaking the string into two smaller strings and using the line continuation character to tell REXX that the rest of the string is found on the next line.   In this example, the comma (,) gets included in the string, which may cause a problem for the program at a later point.

```
/* example e */
say 'example_e:'
say 'this is string 5,


and continuation 5'
```

produces:

this is string 5,   and continuation 5

Figure 5. Invalid use of line continuation.

The error in Fig. 5 is caused by REXX's searching on subsequent lines for the closing quote for the character string. One blank will be included in the string for each of the two blank lines that separate the beginning and ending parts of the character string.

Recommendation: Follow the method shown in Fig. 1.   If you have a character string that is to be continued on the next line in your program, break the string into two smaller strings.   Place the ending quote on the first line, then use the comma to tell REXX that the line is continued on the next line.   Start the character string on the second line with a quote.   This will ensure that

REXX will process the data you intend to be processed. If you do not want the extra space (which comes as part of the "package" with line continuation), use the Concatenation symbol (||) before the comma. This will cause REXX to ignore the blank that would normally become part of the expression or string that was continued.

1.2 Quotes in REXX

The use of quotes in REXX execs has proved to be a stumbling block for many people. Quotes are used in conjunction with many of the REXX instructions (SAY, IF, ARG, TRACE, SELECT, PUSH, QUEUE, PARSE, etc.), as well as most of the built-in functions, and also for host commands (non-REXX statements). However, there are only a few simple rules concerning the use of quotes:

1. REXX allows single or double quotes for each string used in a statement. The first type of quote encountered becomes the "quotes used" for that string; if the "other" quote is encountered, it is simply treated as a character, not a quote (this allows for an easier implementation of an apostrophe, for example).

```
/**/
pull x .
⋮
say "There are four of Rhonda's game scores left on table "||x
```

Figure 6. Mixing quotes in a statement.

Making use of rule 1 for quotes allows the above figure to be used when an apostrophe is desired as part of a string. REXX does not look at this statement and think "there is an odd number of quotes in this statement"; instead, REXX looks at the statement and thinks "there is an apostrophe between the set of quotes..."

2. Quotes are grouped in a "left-to-right" mode, not an "outside-to-inside" mode (parentheses are outside-to-inside).

```
/**/
pull x y .
  :
/* display distance in terms of feet and inches */
say 'The distance turns out to be'||x||"'"||y||'"'
```

Figure 7. Mixing quotes in a statement.

Using rule 2 for quotes, the statement is looked at as follows: the first character string is **The distance turns out to be**; the second string is a single quote (,); the third string is a double quote ("). When these strings are concatenated with the values of x and y, the resulting statement looks like this on output:

```
The distance turns out to be 3'5"
```

3. Anything not contained in a pair of quotes is treated as a variable (in the case of alphabetic characters), or as an operator (in the case of special characters: + - / * = etc.).

```
/**/
list=3
  :
EXEC LIST * SYSPROC B
```

Figure 8. Not using quotes.

This example contains two "errors." The first is that the word LIST will be treated as a variable and will be evaluated to "3"; the second is the asterisk, which will be looked at as the multiplication operator. The arithmetic operation will be carried out before the statement is turned over to the host environment. By using one set of quotes and turning the entire statement into a character string, all of this ambiguity is removed, and the statement will process properly. The statement should be changed to read:

```
'EXEC LIST * SYSPROC B'
```

4. One "level" of quotes is removed from the statement when it is evaluated. If you want to leave a set of quotes, use the "other" quotes as the second set.

```
QUEUE 'the quotes around "next" will be placed on the stack also'
```

Figure 9. Using quotes within quotes.

This example ties in with rule 1. Here, it can be seen that the line of characters that is placed on the Program Stack will have the double quotes around the word next.

Extra attention should be paid if you are using an equal sign (=) as part of the expression of an INTERPRET statement or a SAY statement. If a second set of quotes (of the other kind) is not used around the equal sign (=), it will be treated as the comparative operator '='. The result of this comparison will always be either a "1" or a "0". If, in fact, a literal is desired, then the "other" quotes should surround the equal sign, but remain *within* the quoted string.

Recommendation: When coding your REXX programs, place all nonvariable items in quotes (this, of course, does not apply to numerics). In so doing, you will be saving some additional processing by REXX, for strings not in quotes will be evaluated as variables. Not using quotes can be quite costly, in terms of performance. This does place an additional burden on the part of the programmer, but the increase in readability should help to counter that burden.

1.3 Semicolons in REXX

Many high-level programming languages require a rather extensive use of the semicolon (;) as a statement-end character. REXX allows the programmer to use semicolons to a very great extent, or to use none at all; it is up to the programmer's personal style.

REXX has only one rule concerning semicolons—they must be used if more than one physical line in a program will contain more than one statement. In Fig. 10, a simple program is shown in two different ways (the first without semicolons, in a vertical fashion; the second with semicolons, in a one-line fashion).

```
/* sample program  A */
x=2
y=3
say 'The sum of' x 'and' y 'is' x+y

can be written as


/* sample program B */x=2;y=3;say 'The sum of' x 'and' y 'is' x+y
```

Figure 10. Using semicolons in REXX.

Using a small program like this for illustration purposes might not bring out the important reasons for using (or not using) semicolons, but think of it in terms of a rather large program. Using semicolons can allow you to "pack" statements into a smaller area, from a storage point of view.   However, coding following the style of sample program B does not lend itself to internal documentation capability, nor does it lend itself to being very easily read by someone editing the program.

Exception:

There are two exceptions to the rule for semicolons...the first concerns the IF statement. If the ELSE "leg" is to be included on the same physical line in the program, it must be preceded by a semicolon. The second concerns the use of a DO...END structure following a THEN or an ELSE. If you are going to have the "first instruction inside a Do Group" on the same line as the DO, that instruction must be preceded by a semicolon.

Some high-level languages have allowed the use of the semicolon after a THEN or an ELSE to provide a null leg, or null branch. REXX has provided the NOP instruction for this purpose. REXX will not recognize ELSE; to mean that nothing is to be processed if the condition tested is false... ELSE NOP is what REXX would expect to see in this case. The same applies to the THEN, also.

Recommendation: If your coding style is to "one-line" your REXX programs, then you need to use semicolons extensively. If your coding style is more of a vertical style (this is the more widely used style), then avoid using semicolons unless two or more statements are going to be used on the same physical line of the program. It is quite common for programmers to write several REXX programs without using any semicolons.

1.4 Mixed Case vs. UPPER CASE

One of the programming factors that affects the readability of the program is the use of mixed case versus the use of upper case. Readability of a program is very important if the program is to be modified (enhanced, perhaps) at some time in the future, be it by the programmer or by another person. The time saved in understanding the program's logic and the degree to which the program can be understood can be increased by a consistent approach to the coding of the program statements.

Many high-level languages force the programmer to write all statements in upper case. This facilitates the decision of use of case for program statements. REXX is designed to be flexible in this area; REXX supports mixed-case as well as upper-case coding. The text editor used to create the program is another factor in the question of which case you will be using for your program. Most, if not all, editors allow the programmer to control how characters are typed in (upper case or not).

Figures 11 to 14 show the program MYBANK using different coding schemes concerning case; the first will be all lower case, the second will use upper case for the host commands, the third will go one step further by capitalizing each REXX keyword, and the fourth will be in all upper-case characters. A comparison of the four styles will follow.

```
/*----------------------------------------------------------------/
/-  A program to convert from one currency to another...     -/
/----------------------------------------------------------------*/
call initialize
say 'this program will allow you to convert any of the following'
say 'currencies to another.  please enter the amount:'
pull amount .
say 'the currency units are identified by the number in the list.'
say 'enter the from currency and the to currency with a space between'
say '(for example, 1 3 to convert from USA to pounds):'
do i = 1 to words(currency.list)
   say left(i||'.',3) word(currency.list,i)
end
pull from to
from_currency=word(currency.list,from)
to_currency=word(currency.list,to)
select
  when from=1 then call convert_to_foreign to
  when to=1   then call convert_from_foreign from
  otherwise
    call convert_from_foreign from
    call convert_to_foreign to
end
Say 'the value in 'word(currency.list,to)'s is 'result
exit
initialize:
'execio * diskr currency table (stem line.'
do table_ct=1 to line.0
   interpret line.table_ct
end
return
convert_to_foreign:
arg code
unit=words(currency.list,code)
return amount*currency.unit
convert_from_foreign:
arg code
unit=word(currency.list,code)
return amount/currency.unit
```

Figure 11. MYBANK EXEC—all lower case.

```
/*----------------------------------------------------------------/
/-  A program to convert from one currency to another...      -/
/---------------------------------------------------------------*/
call initialize
say 'this program will allow you to convert any of the following'
say 'currencies to another.  please enter the amount:'
pull amount .
say 'the currency units are identified by the number in the list.'
say 'enter the from currency and the to currency with a space between'
say '(for example, 1 3 to convert from usa to pounds):'
do i = 1 to words(currency.list)
   say left(i||'.',3) word(currency.list,i)
end
pull from to
from_currency=word(currency.list,from)
to_currency=word(currency.list,to)
select
  when from=1 then call convert_to_foreign to
  when to=1   then call convert_from_foreign from
  otherwise
    call convert_from_foreign from
    call convert_to_foreign to
end
Say 'the value in 'word(currency.list,to)'s is 'result
exit
initialize:
'EXECIO * DISKR CURRENCY TABLE (STEM LINE.'
do table_ct=1 to line.0
   interpret line.table_ct
end
return
convert_to_foreign:
arg code
unit=words(currency.list,code)
return amount*currency.unit
convert_from_foreign:
arg code
unit=word(currency.list,code)
return amount/currency.unit
```

Figure 12. MYBANK   EXEC—lower   case,   except   for   HOST
COMMANDS.

```
/*------------------------------------------------------------/
/-  A program to convert from one currency to another...    -/
/------------------------------------------------------------*/
Call initialize
Say 'this program will allow you to convert any of the following'
Say 'currencies to another.  please enter the amount:'
Pull amount .
Say 'the currency units are identified by the number in the list.'
Say 'enter the from currency and the to currency with a space between'
Say '(for example, 1 3 to convert from USA to pounds):'
Do i = 1 to Words(currency.list)
   Say Left(i||'.',3) Word(currency.list,i)
End
Pull from to
from_currency=Word(currency.list,from)
to_currency=Word(currency.list,to)
Select
  When from=1 Then call convert_to_foreign to
  When to=1   Then call convert_from_foreign from
  Otherwise
    Call convert_from_foreign from
    Call convert_to_foreign to
End
Say 'the value in 'Word(currency.list,to)'s is 'result
Exit
Initialize:
'EXECIO * DISKR CURRENCY TABLE (STEM LINE.'
Do table_ct=1 to line.0
   Interpret line.table_ct
End
Return
Convert_to_foreign:
Arg code
unit=Words(currency.list,code)
Return amount*currency.unit
Convert_from_foreign:
Arg code
unit=Word(currency.list,code)
Return amount/currency.unit
```

Figure 13. MYBANK EXEC—Mixed Case.

```
/*-------------------------------------------------------------/
/-  A PROGRAM TO CONVERT FROM ONE CURRENCY TO ANOTHER...    -/
/-------------------------------------------------------------*/
CALL INITIALIZE
SAY 'THIS PROGRAM WILL ALLOW YOU TO CONVERT ANY OF THE FOLLOWING'
SAY 'CURRENCIES TO ANOTHER.  PLEASE ENTER THE AMOUNT:'
PULL AMOUNT .
SAY 'THE CURRENCY UNITS ARE IDENTIFIED BY THE NUMBER IN THE LIST.'
SAY 'ENTER THE FROM CURRENCY AND THE TO CURRENCY WITH A SPACE BETWEEN'
SAY '(FOR EXAMPLE, 1 3 TO CONVERT FROM USA TO POUNDS):'
DO I = 1 TO WORDS(CURRENCY.LIST)
   SAY LEFT(I||'.',3) WORD(CURRENCY.LIST,I)
END
PULL FROM TO
FROM_CURRENCY=WORD(CURRENCY.LIST,FROM)
TO_CURRENCY=WORD(CURRENCY.LIST,TO)
SELECT
  WHEN FROM=1 THEN CALL CONVERT_TO_FOREIGN TO
  WHEN TO=1   THEN CALL CONVERT_FROM_FOREIGN FROM
  OTHERWISE
    CALL CONVERT_FROM_FOREIGN FROM
    CALL CONVERT_TO_FOREIGN TO
END
SAY 'THE VALUE IN 'WORD(CURRENCY.LIST,TO)'S IS 'RESULT
EXIT
INITIALIZE:
'EXECIO * DISKR CURRENCY TABLE (STEM LINE.'
DO TABLE_CT=1 TO LINE.0
   INTERPRET LINE.TABLE_CT
END
RETURN
CONVERT_TO_FOREIGN:
ARG CODE
UNIT=WORDS(CURRENCY.LIST,CODE)
RETURN AMOUNT*CURRENCY.UNIT
CONVERT_FROM_FOREIGN:
ARG CODE
UNIT=WORD(CURRENCY.LIST,CODE)
RETURN AMOUNT/CURRENCY.UNIT
```

Figure 14. MYBANK EXEC—UPPER CASE.

The first style (all lower case) and the fourth style (all upper case) are the simplest to code; they do not require the use of the shift key when coding.   More importantly, they make it more difficult to distinguish between REXX statements and host commands (the use of quotes is not necessarily enough to make that distinction), and routine names and variable names seem to run together.   On the other hand, the second and third styles do make some distinction between host commands and REXX statements in that the host command is in upper case (the nonvariable portions, that is).   Also, the capitalizing of the REXX keywords (including built-in functions) aids in distinguishing the function names from variable names.   In addition, having lower case for the REXX statements and upper case for the nonvariable portions of the host commands will improve the program's readability in that the host command will STAND OUT amongst several lines of lower-case characters.

Having the host commands in upper case is always a good idea. If the default host command environment is being used, the use of upper case will save some cycles for the host environment, which in many cases will translate the statement to upper case.   If a nondefault environment is being used, the statement should be in upper case anyway, since most nondefault environments do not offer the translation to upper case services that the default environments offer.

Recommendation: Place the nonvariable portions of host commands in UPPER CASE.   Not only will this improve the readability of the program, it will also improve the performance of the program when dealing with the default host command environment.   Keep the remainder of the code in lower case; it reads more easily.   Capitalize or UPPERCASE the routine names to make them stand out better from a readability point of view.

1.5   Indentation of Program Lines

There are many different indentation schemes that people have used to write REXX programs.   Some do not indent at all (this is by far the most difficult to read method of coding); some indent a set amount of columns without regard to what statement is being coded; some use a scheme that varies somewhat.   Some place the DO and END on separate lines; some place them on the same lines as the first and last lines of code.

The reason behind using any kind of indentation scheme is to improve the readability of the program, and to better understand its logic. Which statement(s) is/are subordinate to other statements? What code is contained inside a DO loop? Will these statements be performed when the IF condition is true, or when it is false? These are the types of questions that are at stake here.

REXX is a free-form language; there are no indentation requirements. It is up to the programmer to determine how to indent the program lines. Figures 15 to 18 contain examples of different indentation styles. The first has no indentation (each line starts in column 1); the second has an indentation scheme of one column per "level"; the third has a scheme of two to three columns per level, with the DO following the IF or the ELSE; the fourth is similar to the third, but the DO is on a line by itself. A discussion follows the examples.

```
if rstatus = 'PF3' then exit
if rstatus = 'ENTER' then do
do i=1 to 5
address command 'EXECIO 1 DISKR 'infile' (VAR ANSWER'
interpret 'upper ' D||i
right=0
interpret 'if 'D||i' ='answer' then right=1'
if right then num_right = num_right +1
else num_wrong = num_wrong +1
end
end
else nop
return
:
```

Figure 15. Code example with no indentation.

```
if rstatus = 'PF3' then exit
if rstatus = 'ENTER' then do
 do i=1 to 5
  address command 'EXECIO 1 DISKR 'infile' (VAR ANSWER'
  interpret 'upper ' D||i
  right=0
  interpret 'if 'D||i' ='answer' then right=1'
  if right then num_right = num_right +1
  else num_wrong = num_wrong +1
 end
end
else nop
return
⋮
```

Figure 16. Indentation of one column per level.

```
if rstatus = 'PF3' then exit
if rstatus = 'ENTER' then do
   do i=1 to 5
      address command 'EXECIO 1 DISKR 'infile' (VAR ANSWER'
      interpret 'upper ' D||i
      right=0
      interpret 'if 'D||i' ='answer' then right=1'
      if right
        then num_right = num_right +1
        else num_wrong = num_wrong +1
   end
   end
else nop
return
⋮
```

Figure 17. Indentation of two to three columns per level.

```
if rstatus = 'PF3' then exit
if rstatus = 'ENTER'
  then
    do
      do i=1 to 5
        address command 'EXECIO 1 DISKR 'infile' (VAR ANSWER'
        interpret 'upper ' D||i
        right=0
        interpret 'if 'D||i' ='answer' then right=1'
        if right
          then num_right = num_right +1
          else num_wrong = num_wrong +1
      end
    end
  else nop
return
⋮
```

Figure 18. Indentation of three columns with DOs on separate line.

Figure 15 (with no indentation) is very difficult to read, much less to understand. It is difficult to determine which END belongs to the loop, which belongs to the THEN DO, etc. Figure 16 shows the reader which lines are logically subordinate to previous lines. Figure 17 makes the logical path among the statements clearer by increasing the "white space" on the left. Both Figs. 16 and 17 do have one aspect to them that makes it difficult to understand the relationship between the statements, that being the THEN DO—with the DO on the same line as the THEN, it is difficult to line up the END statements at their proper level of indentation. Figure 18 shows a method where the THEN and DO are each on a separate line. While this method creates a longer vertical program, it more clearly shows how the ENDs line up with the DOs.

If the indentation is getting pretty deep (say, 10 levels or more), perhaps that section should be rewritten into more complex conditions or placed in a subroutine. The question of subroutines and functions is discussed in the next chapter.

Recommendation: Indent your programs two or three columns for each next level of indentation, and place the THENs, ELSEs, DOs, and ENDs on separate lines. This will allow the lines to line up in a vertical fashion, thus allowing the white space to the left of the lines to assist the reader in determining the logic of the program.

1.6   Commenting Your Program

The traditional purpose of including comments in programs has been to assist the program reader, not the program user. Generally speaking, program comments were not to be displayed during a run of the program.   However, REXX has provided a function which now makes that idea an interesting one.   The SOURCELINE function will be used to illustrate this point.

Comments can be included in your program in several different ways.   There can be a prologue-type box comment at the beginning of the program, several in-line comments (to explain each segment of the program, and sometimes each line of the program), smaller box comments at each section of the program, or no comments at all (except for the required comment at the beginning of the file, of course).   Some of the box comments are built with many single-line comments; some are built with a single multiline comment.

The prologue comment box typically explains all the interfaces used by the program, along with a pseudocode-like description of the program's logic.   It can span several pages of printed output or several screens of viewing the program on-line.   This can cause more storage to be used when the program is loaded; this may not be acceptable; in which case perhaps it would be better to keep the functional description of the program in a separate file.

The smaller box comments can be placed throughout the program to explain the different logical sections of the program at those points where the logic is implemented.   This offers some assistance to both the program reader and the program "maintainer" in that the "how" immediately follows the "what" that is described in the box comment.   Unless coding standards mandate single-line comments (or if the program is to be input to another program and interpreted), then it is more efficient to use a single, multiline comment to build a comment box.   With this method, REXX will not have to enter and exit the comment-handling routine several times to handle several adjacent comment lines in the program.

Some programs are commented with in-line comments along the right margin. The comment text parallels the flow of the program statements. With a commenting method such as this, it is advisable to reduce the indentation factor, for the program statements may extend into the comment area, which produces a program that can be difficult to read. In addition, it may be more difficult to add or modify comments as the program is modified.

Recommendation: Use relatively small box comments at the beginning of each routine to describe its function, and at various points along the program where needed. Use a single multiline comment unless the program is to be interpreted by another program (in which case each physical line in your program must be a complete REXX statement or complete comment).

An exception to the recommendation follows. It may be desirable to have an in-program help capability, to explain basic syntax. Figure 19 demonstrates a box comment that can be displayed on the screen when the exec is invoked without input arguments, or with a question mark as the sole (or first) input argument.

```
/*
-----------------------------------------------------------------------------
--                                                                         --
-- COUNTER  is an exec that counts the occurrences of a given string --
--          within a specified file.                                       --
-- To invoke, enter:  COUNTER  fn <ft <fm>> st                             --
--                                                                         --
--              where:  fn = filename of file to be code counted          --
--                      ft = filetype of file    (defaults to EXEC)    --
--                      fm = filemode of file    (defaults to A)       --
--                      st = string to be counted                         --
--                                                                         --
-----------------------------------------------------------------------------
*/
arg fn ft fm string
/* show user help if requested */
if fn = '?' | fn = '' then
  do
    do line=2 to sourceline() while sourceline(line) ¬= '*/'
      say sourceline(line)
    end
  end
else
⋮
```

Figure 19. Using SOURCELINE() and comments to provide help.

Chapter 2.
Overall Structure of
Your Program

In looking at the structure of a REXX program, the question of modularity often arises. Should the program be written as one long program, or should it be modularized—that is, broken up at logical points with certain sections of the program placed into routines? There are some costs in modularizing a program; it is more expensive, in terms of internal instructions, to call a routine instead of having the code in the main path. On the other hand, it can aid in the understanding of the program's logic, because the main control section is raised to a higher, summarizing-like, level, and can be abstracted in an easier manner. Also, it will most likely be easier to enhance the program at a future time if it is logically broken into modules. Some people like to use the rule that a section of code should not exceed one page of printed output in length. Following this could possibly make the program more difficult to understand, for one logical section of the program may actually require a longer length. It is obviously dependent on the particular application, but in general, modularizing a program does more good than harm. In this section, internal and external routines will be discussed, as well as the topic of local versus global variables.

Reminder:

The search order for routines in REXX is:

a. Internal (label found in file)

b. Built-in (supplied as part of REXX)

c. External

2.1 Modularity—Internal Routines

As previously stated, breaking sections of the program at logical points into routines—modularizing —can aid the readability of the program.   Many programmers who have written programs for end users have found that the information needs of the end user group change at times.   Some of these changes require modifications to the program.   The ability to modify the program easily is enhanced by modularity.   Instead of having one long section of code that could span several hundred lines, the program would be easier to understand and write if it were broken down with the first group of lines replaced with a call to a routine (either by using the CALL instruction or by invoking the routine as a function).   The routine is then placed in a later part of the file.   There are two concerns about the physical placement of the routine.   If it is placed in the "middle" of main line code, chances are that it will be executed in turn.   This is due to the syntax of the routine, which is simply a label which is reached only by a function invocation (using parentheses) or by the CALL instruction.   If the routine is enabled simply by dropping or falling into that section of the program, the results could be incorrect.   Placing the routine after the main section will help prevent this.

All internal routines are hand-written; REXX provides a library of built-in functions (perhaps they should be called built-in routines, since they can be CALLed...), but they would not normally require a label and RETURN statement (for this could confuse REXX into thinking the internal label is actually the desired routine).   REXX will allow a routine to be accessed as a function and as a subroutine within the same program; the only difference is whether or not the routine is required to pass back some values or not.   If the routine is to be CALLed, then it is not necessary (from a REXX point of view—from an application point of view, this rule may be different) to pass back data.   If the routine is to be invoked as a function, then the routine is required to return some data on the RETURN statement. Routine names follow the same rule as variable names; they can be 250 characters in length, including the colon (:).   In addition, and somewhat different from most other high-level languages, numeric labels are supported as well as alphanumeric labels.   Thus, the label 2: would be valid.   This could help in structuring programs by allowing reference to a routine by values fed in from a terminal or by some other device or file.

The use of a look-aside buffer for labels should put to rest the fears about an interpreted language consuming too much time to find a label.   At the first routine call or invocation (internal, built-in, or external), REXX will start at the top of the file and scan through the code, looking for the specified label.   As it encounters labels, it stores them along with their address in the look-aside buffer.   REXX keeps track of how far down it has searched, and knows when it has reached the physical end of the program.   On subsequent searches for labels, it will use the look-aside buffer to find the specified routine.

2.1.1 Global versus Local Variables

The handling of variables from a scope point of view has perhaps caused more frustration for programmers than it has caused problems.   The default environment for variables is that all are global; everything's fair game.   The presence of the PROCEDURE instruction changes matters considerably.   With PROCEDURE (which, by the way, should be the first statement following the label), all variables used in the routine are known only to the routine;   no changes or new variables created from within the routine will be known to the caller upon return from the routine. The use of EXPOSE is the key to a "mix and match" environment for variables in REXX.

Passing stemmed variables to a routine is at times a stumbling block.   The easiest way to pass an "array" is to expose the stem. This allows complete access to compound variables with that particular stem from within the called routine, but it also means that the called routine has free rein to modify those variables. This may or may not be a desirable situation.   From a REXX point of view, this is fine; it's the application that has to make that decision.

Internal routines deal with the question of global versus local variables, but external routines do not. All variables are local to an external routine.

2.2 Modularity—External Routines

When considering making use of an external routine (or one of the built-in routines), there are some areas that need to be looked at:

- Language of the external routine.   -
- What about global or local variables?
- How will it be called?
- Should it be loaded into storage first?

2.2.1 Language of the External Routine

External routines must be written in REXX if the filetype is EXEC. If the language to be used is another language (including Assembler), the six-word Extended Plist (parameter list) must be supported.   CMS EXEC and EXEC 2 are not supported for external routines. REXX will assume the routine with filetype of EXEC is written in REXX. One difference between running a REXX program as a stand-alone program (or as a host command) and running a REXX program as an external routine is that the initial comment line is not required for the external routine. This can be used to keep certain external routines within a given application package from being run stand-alone by end users who are not familiar with REXX's processing. Those who are familiar with REXX may be able to get around this pseudo-security.

2.2.2 What about Global or Local Variables?

External routines will always work with Local variables. If the routine is being written in another language (again, not including CMS EXEC or EXEC 2), then the EXECCOMM interface is available to give access to the current REXX program's variables. This gives global variables to the called routine, but they are not "natural" global variables. The EXECCOMM interface must be used to access them.

2.2.3 How Will It Be Called?

If the external routine is to be called as a subroutine (within CMS), it will cost approximately five SVCs (supervisor calls) to access the routine. If the routine is instead treated as a host command, there will be only one or two SVCs. In addition, the external subroutine will make use of the variable RESULT. An external routine as a host command will be able to make use only of the variable RC (and be able to supply only a single numeric value). To be able to return more than one numeric value, or to return character data, you must use the routine as a subroutine or function.

2.2.4 Should It Be Loaded into Storage First?

If the operating environment supports loading the programs into storage prior to execution, take advantage of it. When an external routine is invoked, it is read into storage from disk. This occurs every time that routine is invoked. By loading the programs into storage before the main program is executed, the time required to load the program into storage each subsequent time will no longer be required. This could save a large amount of time.

Chapter 3.
How to Get Pretty Output

The input and output capabilities in REXX are character and/or line oriented. There is no way to get EXECIO or CHAROUT or LINEOUT to follow any particular format when writing to the screen or to a file, in the manner that FORTRAN allows (the FORMAT statement). Instead, the built-in routines that are supplied with REXX may be used to arrange output. Numeric output will be treated separately from character output. Examples will be provided.

3.1 Pretty Output—Numeric Output

When formatting numbers for output to the screen, there are some built-in routines that may be helpful—FORMAT(), TRUNC(), and STRIP(). Some examples follow their discussion. There are additional routines that may be helpful—CENTER(), LEFT(), RIGHT(), etc.; these are discussed in Sec. 3.2, "Character Output."

3.1.1 FORMAT() Function

The FORMAT() function performs the following functions (some of them are optional):

- Rounds the number

- Formats the number within the allocated spaces of the BEFORE and AFTER fields

- Returns the number in Scientific notation

The syntax of the function requires the number first, followed by the number of character positions to allocate for the integer part of the number, the number of character positions to allocate for the decimal part of the number, the number of character positions for the exponent (*if* the number is to be displayed in Scientific notation), and the point at which the number will be returned in Scientific notation (this is determined by the number of character positions needed for the integer portion).

3.1.2 TRUNC() Function

The TRUNC() function performs the following functions (some of them are optional):

- Truncates the number at the decimal point or at the specified decimal place (you can enter the number of decimal digits you want to keep - the default is 0) and returns the number in Scientific notation

- Rounds the number, if necessary (uses NUMERIC DIGITS to do this)

The syntax of the function requires the number first, followed by the number of decimal positions to return in addition to the integer part of the number. If you specify a 0 for the number of decimal places, the decimal point will not be returned. If you specify a value greater than 0, the decimal point is included in the returned value. The number will not be returned in Scientific notation. The rounding of a number when using the TRUNC() function will take place when the number of digits in the number exceeds the setting of NUMERIC DIGITS. For example,

```
a=321.123456789
say trunc(a,8)
```

requests that the number be returned with 8 decimal places displayed. The number of digits in the variable a is 12. This is higher than the default setting for NUMERIC DIGITS (which is 9). The number will be rounded off to 6 decimal places (added to the 3 in the integer part of the number), and then padded with 0's to get the 8 decimal places. The final result from this function call is 321.12345700.

3.1.3 STRIP() Function

The STRIP() function performs the following functions (some of them are optional):

- Removes leading and/or trailing characters from a string (or number)
- Returns the new string (or number)
- Returns the number in Scientific notation

The syntax of the function requires the number first, followed by the stripping option (Leading, Trailing, or Both), followed by the character to be stripped off. You can specify only one character to be stripped. The number will *not* be rounded; it will be treated as a character string. The default option is Both, meaning both leading and trailing characters (that are specified) will be stripped off. The default character is a blank.

3.1.4 Examples of Numeric Output

Suppose you have a report you are producing with your REXX program, and it must match the following format:

```
Item      Quantity  Cost      Total      Conversion   Final
number    sold      per item  cost ($)   factor (%)   cost ($)
-----------------------------------------------------------------
A01        99999    9999.99    99999.99   999.99       999999.99
⋮
A99
```

Here is one way that you can ensure that the numbers produced in the report conform to the predefined format (for the sake of this example, let's assume the numbers are in a "raw data" file, and the file has been read onto the program stack):

```
do i = 1 to 99
   item_number='A'||i
   if i < 10 then item_number = 'A'||'0'||i
   parse pull quantity cost total convert final
   quantity=format(strip(quantity,'L',0),5)
   cost=format(strip(cost,'L',0),4,2)
   total=format(strip(total,'L',0),5,2)
   convert=format(strip(convert,'L',0),3,2)
   final=format(strip(final,'L',0),6,2)
   outline=item_number||'        '||quantity||'   '||cost||,
      '    '||total||'   ||convert||'       '||final
   say outline /* or perhaps print it to a file*/
end
```

It would have been possible to use abuttal concatenation in the
building or the variable outline, but there would have been one
extra blank as a result of the line continuation. Because of this,
the concatenation symbol (||) was used throughout the statement.
The extra blank could have also been compensated for by having
one less blank in the string of blanks on the second line, but that
could have thrown someone off at a later time.

3.2   Pretty Output—Character Output

When formatting character strings for output to the screen, there
are   some   built-in   routines   that   may   be
helpful—CENTER()/CENTRE(), COPIES(), JUSTIFY(), LEFT(),
RIGHT(), SPACE(), and STRIP(). Some examples follow their
discussion. There are additional routines that may also be helpful-
OVERLAY, REVERSE, INSERT, etc.; these will be discussed as a
separate group of routines.

3.2.1   CENTER()/CENTRE() Function

The CENTER() function (it can be spelled either way) performs
the following functions (some of them are optional):

- Centers the string within the specified number of spaces

- Inserts pad character as needed; the default character is a blank

- Returns the new form of the string

The syntax of the function requires the string first, followed by the number of character positions in which to center the string, and the character to be used if padding is necessary. Only one character may be specified as the pad character; it is not to be thought of as a "pad-string" capability.

3.2.2 COPIES() Function

The COPIES() function performs the following functions:

- Repeats the specified string a specified number of times.

- Returns the new string

The syntax of the function requires the string first (which may be contained in a variable), followed by the number of times the string is to be repeated. The number must be a whole number greater than or equal to 0 (zero). Zero is allowed as a number; in this case, the null string will be returned. The length of the string that is returned by the function is not limited by the REXX language; however, the system in which the language is running will most likely have something to say about how long a string of characters referenced by a REXX variable is.

3.2.3 SPACE() Function

The SPACE() function performs the following functions:

- Formats the specified string, leaving the specified number of pad characters between each blank-delimited substring

- Returns the new string

The syntax of the function requires the string first (which may be contained in a variable), followed by the number of pad characters to be included between each blank-delimited substring. The number of pad characters must be a nonnegative whole number (0 is allowed; this will cause all blanks to be removed, and the substrings will be concatenated), and the default pad character

is a blank.   Only one character may be specified as the pad
character; it is not to be thought of as a "pad-string" capability.

3.2.4   JUSTIFY() Function

The JUSTIFY() function performs the following functions:

- Formats the string as if SPACE(string,1,' ') had been specified
- Adds additional pad character between blank-delimited substrings as needed to satisfy the specified length (as long as the length specified is as long as or longer than the result of the first step)
- Replaces the blanks with the specified pad character
- Returns the new string

The syntax of the function requires the string first (which may
be contained in a variable), followed by the length of the final
string in which the initial string is to be justified, and the pad
character that is to be used to separate the blank-delimited
substrings of the initial strings.   The default pad character is a
blank.   There is no default for the length; it must be specified.
Zero is allowed as a length; in this case, the null string will be
returned.   If the specified length is shorter than the result of the
normalizing of the string (the "issuing" of space(string,1,' ')), then
the normalized string is truncated to the specified length, and any
trailing blanks are removed.   The remaining blanks in the string
are then replaced by the pad character.   Therefore, it is possible
to lose some of the characters from the initial string.   The length
of the string that is returned by the function is not limited by the
REXX language; however, the system in which the language is
running will most likely have something to say about how long a
string of characters referenced by a REXX variable may be.

3.2.5   LEFT() Function

The LEFT() function performs the following functions (some of
which are optional):

- Truncates the specified string at the specified character (length)
- Pads the new string on the right with the specified pad character

- Returns the new string

The syntax of the function requires the string first (which may be contained in a variable), followed by the length of the returned string, and the pad character that is to be added to the right of the string if the length specified is greater than the length of the initial string. The length must be specified. The pad character will default to a blank.

3.2.6   RIGHT() Function

The RIGHT() function performs the following functions some of which are optional):

- Truncates the left portion of the initial string to fit into the specified length
- Pads the string on the left with the specified pad character
- Returns the new string′

The syntax of the function requires the string first (which may be contained in a variable), followed by the length of the new string, and the pad character to be used if the specified length is greater than the length of the initial string. Any leading blanks in the initial string will not be converted to the pad character. The default pad character is a blank.

3.2.7   STRIP() Function

The STRIP() function performs the following functions (some of which are optional):

- Removes leading and/or trailing characters from a string (or number)
- Returns the new string (or number)
- Returns the number in Scientific notation

The syntax of the function requires the number first, followed by the stripping option (Leading, Trailing, or Both), followed by the character to be stripped off. You can specify only one character to be stripped. The number will *not* be rounded; it will be treated as a character string. The default option is Both, meaning both leading and trailing characters (that are specified) will be stripped off. The default character is a blank.

3.2.8 Examples of Character Output

Suppose you have a report you are producing with your REXX program, and it must match the following format:

```
---------1---------2---------3---------4---------5---------6---------
Member     Member     Phone      Supervisor   Current    Performance
Name       Dept.      Number     Name         Project    Report Due?
---------------------------------------------------------------------
Reinhold   X23 4G     123-4567   Kiesel       HRDOK           *
:
```

Here is one way that the headings and data fields can line up when this report is produced:

```
/* let's assume all records are on the program stack          */
headline1=copies('Member     ',2)||left('Phone',12)||,
          left('Supervisor',13)||left('Current',11)||'Performance'
headline2=copies('Name',11)||left('Dept.',11)||left('number',12)||,
          center('Name',13)||left('Project',11)||'Report Due?'
separator=copies('-',69)
    :
say headline1; say headline2; say separator
do i = 1 to queued()
   parse member phone dept_minor dept_major super curr_proj due
   outline=left(member,11)||left(space(dept_minor dept_major),10)||,
           left(number,13)||left(super,13)||left(curr_project,11)||,
           center(strip(due,'B',' '),11)
   if i//5=0 then say separator
   say outline /*or perhaps write it out to a file*/
end
```

It would have been possible to use abuttal concatenation in the building or the variable outline, but there would have been one extra blank as a result of the line continuation. Because of this, the concatenation symbol (||) was used throughout the statement. The extra blank could have also been compensated for by having one less blank in the string of blanks on the second line, but that could have thrown someone off at a later time.

Chapter 4.
Programming Tricks

As you have written REXX programs, no doubt you have begun to develop your own coding style. You may prefer to use a SELECT statement instead of using several nested IF statements; you may prefer to use CALL to access internal routines as opposed to using the function interface; you may even choose to use CALL to get to the library of built-in functions. REXX's flexibility is to be thanked for this.

As you get more and more familiar with REXX's capabilities, you might begin to notice some subtle characteristics of the language that seem to become handy in certain cases. Some of these are discussed in this section. The word "tricks" as it is used in this book is not meant in the negative sense, but rather in the "hey, that's kinda neat" sense. Here are some of the "tricks" that have been found:

4.1 Use of VALUE (or Variable Name) instead of INTERPRET

The INTERPRET instruction is by far one of the more powerful, if not the most misunderstood, of the REXX instructions. It enforces a type of "backwards" thinking. It is used to create both REXX instructions and host commands (non-REXX statements). In the latter case, some have found that there are other ways to execute host commands from within a REXX program. The trick here lies in the understanding of how statements are executed by REXX... Figure 20 demonstrates alternatives to using the INTERPRET instruction to execute a host command.

```
/*------------------------------------------------------------/
/- For this example, let's assume that a data record has    -/
/- a particular host command associated with a particular   -/
/- code.  Upon entering the code from the terminal, the     -/
/- command will be executed when a match is made on the code.-/
/------------------------------------------------------------*/
code.=''
code.1='CP MSG BILL time for coffee?'
code.2='CP FORCE BILL'
code.3='EXEC ABC'
   :
say 'Please enter the code:'
parse pull code .
if command.code ¬= ''
   then interpret command.code";say rc"    /* interpret method */
   :
if command.code ¬= ''
   then value(command.code);say rc         /* value() method   */
   :
if command.code ¬= ''
   then command.code;say rc                /* variable method  */
   :
if command.code ¬= ''
   then ''command.code;say rc              /* "" method        */
```

Figure 20. Programming trick—alternatives to INTERPRET.

The INTERPRET method is one that has been used by many to execute a host command. It functions based on the function of the INTERPRET instruction. No tricks here; just straightforward use of INTERPRET (which could be not-so-straightforward to some).

The VALUE() method makes use of a subtle point in REXX's processing of statements. The data string returned from a function is made part of the statement that contained the function call. Since the statement consists of the function only, the result of the statement is then treated as a host command, and is passed to the appropriate host command environment. This seems to violate one of the "rules" regarding the use of function calls, namely, that a function should not stand alone as a separate statement in a REXX program. The reason for this is that the result from a function may not actually be a valid host command; instead, it is more likely a data string for use in the program. However, the fact that the function as a statement alone can have its result treated as a host command provides some benefit as an alternative to the use of the INTERPRET instruction.

The VARIABLE method is similar to the VALUE() method, but the idea of getting at the value inside the variable is perhaps more clearly shown; variables are most commonly used to hold a value that can be used when the variable is evaluated. As REXX is interpreting the statement to decide how to process it, the last step before treating it as a host command is to evaluate any and all variables in the statement, building a string of characters which then get passed to a host command environment. This is how the variable **command.code** is being used in this example.

The " method is using a not-really-all-that-subtle aspect of REXX's recognizing of host commands. This is just another way of coding a host command in REXX. It tells REXX that the statement is a host command, and once the evaluations of any variables are made, sends the statement to the active host command environment to be executed.

All of the above methods will work when the statement being built is a host command. If the statement being built contains arithmetic operators or REXX instructions (DO, SAY, SELECT, etc.), then the INTERPRET instruction should be used.

4.2 Advanced Parsing Techniques—Multiple Assignment

Have you ever wanted to assign the same value to several simple variables but did not look forward to having several ____ = ____ statements? Well, REXX has a way of accomplishing this that not only is easy to maintain, but also is more efficient than having several assignment statements...

The PARSE instruction allows this through the use of absolute character position on the template. For example, the statement in Fig. 21 will assign a blank to each of the variables in the template. This is accomplished by using the character position 1 between each variable. In essence, the template is telling the PARSE instruction to "go back to character position 1 of the data being parsed, and place the complete string into this variable."

```
    ⋮
parse value ' ' with 1 abc 1 XYZ 1 DEF 1 GHI 1 JLK 1 X 1 Y 1 N 1 Z
    ⋮
```

Figure 21. Programming trick—multiple assignment using PARSE.

You are not limited to assigning only one character to several variables, nor are you limited to using only a blank. Any value will work.

4.3 Use of INDEX/POS/FIND/WORDPOS

Quite often, a list of values is searched for a match on a particular character string. This is one method of verifying the validity of input parameters to a program. For example, if Program A accepts an input parameter that could be one of several values, it is not uncommon to see code like Fig. 22.

```
/*-------------------------------------------------------------/
/- valid inputs are: APPEnd, APPly, NOTRANS, TRANS...       -/
/-------------------------------------------------------------*/
   :
parse arg input .
   :
routine_loc = pos(input,'APPEND APPLY NOTRANS TRANS')
select
  when routine_loc=1 then call append_routine
  when routine_loc=2 then call apply_routine
  when routine_loc=3 then call trans_routine 'NO'
  when routine_loc=4 then call trans_routine 'YES'
  otherwise call issue_error_message
end
   :
```

Figure 22. Programming trick—searching values using POS/INDEX.

However, upon running this example, it is soon discovered that there is a problem— it doesn't work.The POS function is a string-searching function, as opposed to a word-searching function. The string APPLY is found at position 8, which would be assigned to the variable routine_loc. You can see what effect this would have on the program. Ok, so we change the values inside the select statement. Now when the program is run, another problem emerges: when APP is entered as an abbreviation for APPLY, the string will be found in APPEND (the same goes for TRANS; it would be found in NOTRANS) first...

4.4 Advanced Parsing Techniques—Issuing CP Commands

In addition to the multiple assignment using the PARSE instruction, there are some other ways in which the PARSE instruction can be used that may not be straightforward.

When issuing CP commands from your program, it is more efficient to make use of the PARSE instruction in the following manner:

```
parse value diag(8,'CP QUERY DASD') with ....... '15'x .......
```

This will capture the output response from the CP QUERY command and will allow you to access each line of output, because of the end-of-line character ('15'x) being used a a literal matching pattern.   If the number of output response lines is not known, then the string can be processed in a loop that parses the string on the '15'x and ends when the string is empty ('').

Part 2.
How to Debug
Your Program

Chapter 5.
The TRACE Instruction

From time to time, there will be programs that you will either write or read or be given to maintain, and a question may arise as to how a particular section (or routine) of a program *actually* works... The program may or may not have many internal comments (there will, of course, be at least one—the first line of the program must start with a comment), or it may only have some external functional documentation (describing what it produces, without much to describe how it processes the data it uses). The ideal setup is to have a program with adequate internal and external documentation, but how often does this happen? There are many reasons for using the information in this chapter, perhaps for the reasons stated above, or perhaps simply to satisfy a curiosity of how a particular program works... whatever the reason, this chapter can provide assistance.

This chapter highlights the TRACE instruction for the purpose of investigating a (section of a) program. Two methods of tracing a program will be discussed. In addition, this chapter highlights commonly found errors that have occurred when people write EXECs (programs) using REXX. It is useful to those who are responsible for testing REXX programs for accuracy and/or efficiency, as to those who read or write REXX programs, allowing the program reader/writer/tester to "learn by others' mistakes."

5.1   The TRACE Instruction—General

There can be as many TRACE instructions in your program as you feel are necessary (and then some).   A different alphabetic and/or prefix option may be used each time the TRACE instruction is encountered.   TRACEing can be turned off at any point in your code (see Fig. 23).   REXX provides the TRACE instruction to facilitate the debugging of a REXX program.   It controls how much information is shown on the terminal when the program is running.

```
/*-----------------------------------------------------------/
/- program fragment to illustrate tracing...              -/
/- call three subroutines to gather, sort, and report...  -/
/----------------------------------------------------------*/
call gather_data
TRACE I          /* trace the sort_data routine only */
call sort_data
TRACE 'OFF'      /* turn tracing off */
call report_data
```

Figure 23. Tracing only a part of your program.

5.1.1   Alphabetic Options

There are many alphabetic character options available for use by the TRACE instruction; the ones that will be discussed here are

> Results

> Intermediates

> Labels

5.1.1.1   Tracing the RESULT of a statement

This level of tracing will show the result of the processing performed by REXX.   In Fig. 24, TRACE R is used to show how the trace output can be used to better understand how the program executes.

```
/*---------------------------------------------------------------/
/- ask a question, and check the answer...                     -/
/---------------------------------------------------------------*/
TRACE R
answer= 'IT'
say 'I am thinking of a word that has 26 letters...'
say 'how is it spelled?'
pull response .
if response = answer
  then say 'correct. You sure are sharp to catch that one'
  else say 'close, but I was looking for ->' answer '<-'
Exit
```

Figure 24. Example using TRACE R.

Figure 24 produces the result shown in Fig. 25.

```
      5 *-* answer= 'IT'
       >>>    "IT"
      6 *-* say 'I am thinking of a word that has 26 letters...'
       >>>    "I am thinking of a word that has 26 letters..."
I am thinking of a word that has 26 letters...
      7 *-* say 'how is it spelled?'
       >>>    "how is it spelled?"
how is it spelled?
      8 *-* pull response .
antidisestablishmentarianism
       >>>    "ANTIDISESTABLISHMENTARIANISM"
       >.>    ""
      9 *-* if response = answer
       >>>    "0"
     11 *-* else
      *-*    say 'close, but I was looking for ->' answer '<-'
       >>>    "close, but I was looking for -> IT <-"
close, but I was looking for -> IT <-
     12 *-* Exit
```

Figure 25. Example of TRACE R output.

Here, you see each statement that is executed and the result of the processing done on that statement. The first statement following the TRACE instruction is the statement ANSWER = 'IT'. When traced, it comes out in the form

```
5 *-* answer= 'IT'
  >>>   "IT"
```

The *-* identifies the statement being traced. The >>> identifies the trace output; in this example, the value IT is being assigned to the variable ANSWER. Using TRACE R in your program helps you to better understand what REXX is doing with a particular statement (or group of statements) in your program. An interesting point to make here is that the output of the TRACE instruction will appear on the terminal the same way that the output from a SAY instruction does. You see the output that would have been produced, plus the trace output.

5.1.1.2 Tracing the INTERMEDIATE parts of a statement.

This level of tracing will show the result of the processing performed by REXX. The following example uses TRACE I to display more detailed information as the statement is being executed.

```
/*------------------------------------------------------------/
/- ask a question, and check the answer...                  -/
/------------------------------------------------------------*/
TRACE I
answer= 'IT'
say 'I am thinking of a word that has 26 letters in it...'
say 'how is it spelled?'
pull response .
if response = answer
  then say 'correct. You sure are sharp to catch that one'
  else say 'close, but I was looking for ->' answer '<-'
Exit
```

Figure 26. Example using TRACE I.

Figure 26 produces the result shown in Fig. 27.

```
   5 *-* answer= 'IT'
     >L>   "IT"
   6 *-* say 'I am thinking of a word that has 26 letters...'
     >L>   "I am thinking of a word that has 26 letters..."
I am thinking of a word that has 26 letters...
   7 *-* say 'how is it spelled?'
     >L>   "how is it spelled?"
how is it spelled?
   8 *-* pull response .
antidisestablishmentarianism
     >>>   "ANTIDISESTABLISHMENTARIANISM"
     >.>   ""
   9 *-* if response = answer
     >V>   "ANTIDISESTABLISHMENTARIANISM"
     >V>   "IT"
     >O>   "0"
  11 *-* else
     *-*   say 'close, but I was looking for ->' answer '<-'
     >L>   "close, but I was looking for ->"
     >V>   "IT"
     >O>   "close, but I was looking for -> IT"
     >L>   "<-"
     >O>   "close, but I was looking for -> IT <-"
close, but I was looking for -> IT <-
  12 *-* Exit
```

Figure 27. Example of TRACE I output.

Here, you not only see each statement that is executed, but you also see how REXX resolves the intermediate steps in that statement. For example, the first statement following the TRACE instruction is the statement ANSWER = 'IT'. When traced, it comes out in the form

```
   5 *-* answer= 'IT'
     >L>   "IT"
```

The *-* identifies the statement being traced. The >?> identifies the trace output. In addition, the "L" indicates that the value "IT" comes from a literal string (it could also come from an uninitialized variable). If the statement had been ANSWER = Y, the trace output would have shown a >V>, identifying the value "IT" as coming from a variable. The trace output of statement 9 illustrates this point. The statement is "looked at" by REXX in a left-to-right fashion. The first > V > identifies the variable RESPONSE, and the second > V > identifies the variable ANSWER. The > O > identifies the result of an operation (in this case, a comparison for strings being equal). The last line of trace output is exactly what you would see on a > > > line from TRACE R, but TRACE I goes one step further in giving the CHARACTER code between the two > 's. Take a look back at the trace output for TRACE I and compare it with the trace output for TRACE R. The use of TRACE I gives much more information than TRACE R, and is strongly recommended; when you are interested in seeing how a particular statement works (or a group of statements), why not get all the information you can?

5.1.1.3 Tracing the Labels encountered during the run of a program

This level of tracing will show the labels encountered by REXX.

```
/*----------------------------------------------------------------/
/- program fragment to illustrate tracing...                    -/
/- the second subroutine will be called only if answer=2...     -/
/----------------------------------------------------------------*/
TRACE L              /* trace all labels during this run */
call gather_data
if answer=2 then call sort_data
call report_data
exit
gather_data:
answer=1
return
sort_data:
'EXECUTE SORT_DATA'
return
report_data:
say answer
return
```

Figure 28. Example of using TRACE LABELS.

Figure 28 produces the result shown in Fig. 29.

```
test2
    10 *-*  gather_data:
    16 *-*  report_data:
1
Ready;
```

Figure 29. Tracing only a part of your program.

Here, you see only two types of output: the "normal" program
output (in this case from the SAY statement), and the trace output
which shows the program labels that are explicitly referenced
during this run of the program.   It is important to note the
absence of the sort_data label; since the variable ANSWER
contained a "1" after the call to gather_data, it was clear that the
sort_data routine would not be run.   However, in the search for
the report_data routine, REXX had to notice that the label
"sort_data:" was in the program also.   REXX noticed it, but since
it was not the one it was looking for, it did not produce the label
as part of the trace output. The trace output for TRACE L shows
a functional progression through routines in a program, not the
physical progression through the program file (of course, the
physical order of the routines is entirely up to the programmer).

5.1.2 Prefix Options

There are also two prefix options that can be specified on the
TRACE instruction:

  ! - which **inhibits the execution of host commands**

  ? - which provides **interactive debugging** capability

These prefix options may be combined on the same TRACE
instruction.   One alphabetic option may be specified, but it may be
combined with one or both of the prefix options. If a prefix option
is used with an alphabetic character option, there may not be any
blanks between the options, and the prefix option(s) must precede
the alphabetic option.   For example, to trace a program
interactively at the Intermediates level, also inhibiting host
commands, the TRACE instruction should look like:

```
TRACE ?!I
```

Note: Prefix options may be specified in any order. The prefix character may also be used by itself on the TRACE instruction. Each time a prefix option is used, it will reverse the action of that prefix (similar to an on/off switch).

5.1.2.1 (!) Inhibiting the execution of host commands

The inhibiting of host commands works this way: the command

```
TRACE !I
```

will cause any host commands (e.g., CP or CMS commands) to *not* be executed. (If the ! were not used, the commands would be executed and the variable RC would be set to the value of the return code.) The REXX variable RC will be set to "0", as if the command had executed and returned a return code of 0. The program will then continue to execute. This is helpful to test the "good" paths inside a program.

Note: There *is* a drawback to this, however. There may be times that a nonzero value is expected from a particular command (a return code value of 28 from the CMS STATE command indicates that a certain file does not exist on the specified disk(s); this may not be considered an "error" to a particular program); in a case such as this, the use of the ! prefix option is not encouraged.

5.1.2.2 (?) Interactive debugging of your program.

The interactive debugging of your program works this way: the command

```
TRACE ?I
```

will cause REXX to stop after each clause (part of a statement) has executed. When the Enter key is pressed, REXX will then proceed with the next clause (each block of comment lines will be treated as one clause). While this causes the program to run slower, it allows you to closely watch how the program is processing.

5.2 Trace Instruction—"Straight"

The preceding examples of TRACE have been in noninteractive mode.   This "straight" mode involves editing the program and inserting one or more TRACE instructions in the program, at predetermined points.   The TRACE instruction can be coded to make use of the TRACE VALUE x capability;   this trace setting can then be triggered during a later run by (perhaps) specifying a particular input argument to the program, or perhaps by setting the value in some file to be used by the program as a profile. Figure 30 shows the use of a "dormant TRACE," that is, a TRACE instruction that can be triggered by an input parameter.

```
/*---------------------------------------------------------------/
/- program fragment to illustrate tracing...                 -/
/- call three subroutines to gather, sort, and report...     -/
/----------------------------------------------------------*/
arg trace_setting
(some code to ensure a valid trace setting is entered)
   :
call gather_data
TRACE VALUE trace_setting /* trace the sort_data routine */
call sort_data
TRACE 'OFF'          /* turn tracing off */
call report_data
```

Figure 30. The "dormant TRACE".

When this program is run, an input argument of "I" could be entered, which would cause the sort_data routine to be traced at the Intermediates level.   Tracing would be turned off when the program encountered the TRACE OFF after the sort_data routine ended.   This technique is helpful in cases where new routines are being added to a particular program during its life cycle of use, and many of those added routines will affect some of the data processing done in the traced program sections (or routines).   This makes future modifications to the code easier to test when they are added.

5.3 TRACE Instruction—Interactive

The "interactive" mode of tracing involves the use of the prefix option ?. The TRACE instruction can be inserted into the file at any point, similar to the "straight" mode of TRACE. In addition, some of the operating environments which support REXX (such as CMS) allow the initiation of interactive tracing from outside the program. The example of this which this section will refer to is the SET EXECTRAC command, which is a CMS command (it came into being with Release 4 of CMS). The use of the SET EXECTRAC command will be shown in the following example.

The use of TRACE in interactive mode offers a great deal of flexibility to the REXX program writer. The ability to control the pace of the displaying of the trace output allows the programmer to follow the control of logic without being bothered by additional statements appearing on the screen while trying to concentrate on a particular statement. Yet another aspect of interactive tracing's flexibility is the ability of the programmer to enter various inputs while "between" statements.

While in interactive mode, there are several types of inputs to choose from:

- A null line (just press Enter), which will cause the next statement to be executed.

- An equal sign (=), which will cause the last statement executed to be re-executed.

- A TRACE instruction, which will cause REXX to change the tracing option in effect to the new option.

- A TRACE instruction (with an integer value), which will save you having to press Enter "n" times. For example,

```
TRACE 10
```

will display the trace output that you would see if you had pressed Enter 10 times, but it would show the output all at once.

- Another REXX instruction, which will be executed before the next program statement is executed. The new statement must be a COMPLETE statement (i.e., DO ... END and IF-THEN-ELSE constructs must be complete).

- A host command, which will be executed before the next program statement is executed. The host command will not place its return code in the special variable RC in this case; only host commands in the program will place a return code in RC.

The following program, MYBANK EXEC, will be used to illustrate interactive tracing. It has a companion file, CURRENCY TABLE, which acts as an "include" file or macro, by use of the INTERPRET instruction. This program is run in CMS; hence the use of the file name and file type (in TSO, this would be the ddname) in the EXECIO command. The program will be shown without any bugs in it, but the running of the program will be shown with a version that has bugs, in order to demonstrate interactive tracing and how it helps you to debug a program.

```
/* The table contains the value of foreign currencies in */
/* relation to the U.S. Dollar                           */
currency.list='USA YEN POUND MARK FRANC CANADIAN LIRE'
currency.usa=1
currency.yen=125
currency.pound=.57687
currency.franc=6.15
currency.canadian=1.25
currency.lire=1342
```

Figure 31. CURRENCY TABLE used by the MYBANK program.

```
/*--------------------------------------------------------------/
/-  A program to convert from one currency to another...     -/
/--------------------------------------------------------------*/
call initialize
say 'This program will allow you to convert any of the following'
say 'currencies to another.  Please enter the amount:'
pull amount .              .
say 'The currency units are identified by the number in the list.'
say 'ENTER the FROM currency and the TO currency, separated by a'
say 'blank (for example, 1 3 to convert from USA to POUNDs):'
do i = 1 to words(currency.list)
   say left(i||'.',3) word(currency.list,i)
end
pull from to
from_currency=word(currency.list,from)
to_currency=word(currency.list,to)
select
  when from=1 then call convert_to_foreign to
  when to=1   then call convert_from_foreign from
  otherwise
    call convert_from_foreign from
    call convert_to_foreign to
end
Say 'the value in 'word(currency.list,to)'s is 'result
exit
initialize:
'EXECIO * DISKR CURRENCY TABLE (STEM LINE.'
do table_ct=1 to line.0
   interpret line.table_ct
end
return
convert_to_foreign:
arg code
unit=word(currency.list,code)
return amount*currency.unit
convert_from_foreign:
arg code
unit=word(currency.list,code)
return amount/currency.unit
```

Figure 32. MYBANK program to illustrate interactive debug.

Figures 33 through 37 show how interactive tracing can be helpful when debugging a program. The output is from a sample CMS session; the lines entered while in Interactive Debug mode are highlighted. The figures show logical "breakpoints", with a discussion following each figure.

```
mybank  1
This program will allow you to convert any of the following
currencies to another.  Please enter the amount:
25.00
The currency units are identified by the number in the list.
ENTER the FROM currency and the TO currency with a space between
(for example, 1 3 to convert from USA to POUNDs):
1 3
1.  USA
2.  YEN
3.  POUND
4.  MARK
5.  FRANC
6.  CANADIAN
7.  LIRE
the value in POUNDs is 14.4217500        2
Ready;
```

Figure 33. MYBANK program to illustrate interactive debug.

The first run of MYBANK EXEC, example parts **1** and **2**, show a normal run with clean code. Let's see what we can do when running a version of the program with some bugs in it...

```
mybank  3
  28 +++    do table_ct=1 to line.0
   4 +++ call initialize
DMSREX476E Error 41 running MYBANK EXEC, line 28: Bad arithmetic conversion
Ready(20041);
set exectrac on   4
Ready;
```

Figure 34. MYBANK program—noticing something is wrong.

Example part **3** shows what happens when the "bugged" version is run. REXX produces one or more error messages, and halts the running of the program. The purpose of this example is to demonstrate interactive tracing, so let's do it by issuing the SET EXECTRAC ON command (a CMS command; see example part **4**).

The SET EXECTRAC ON command was chosen as the way to initiate tracing the program. The TRACE ?R command could have been placed in the code itself; this would have given us the same capability the "outside the code" command gives us. However, there are some programming environments that may preclude the modification of the code (even to put in something as simple as a TRACE instruction); the SET EXECTRAC ON command allows us to "get at" the code from the outside.

```
mybank    5
     +++ "CMS COMMAND MYBANK EXEC A1 mybank CMS"
   1 *-* /*-------------------------------------------------------------//-
program to convert from one currency to another...    -//------------------
-------------------------------------*/
   4 *-* call initialize
  26 *-* initialize:
     +++ Interactive trace. TRACE OFF to end debug, ENTER to continue. ++
trace ?1   6
  28 +++   do table_ct=1 to line.0
   4 +++ call initialize
DMSREX476E Error 41 running MYBANK EXEC, line 28: Bad arithmetic conversion
Ready(20041);
```

Figure 35. MYBANK program—running with Interactive Trace.

Running the program again (**5**), we now get some additional statements, and the program stops *after* the first executable statement. At this point, a different level of tracing may be specified (example part **6**). Here, a tracing level of Labels is selected. However, the presence of the label initialize: before we have a chance to change the tracing level indicates that we were already in the routine that we want. The answer still may not be very clear, so let's go back at it again, and try something different.

```
set exectrac on
Ready;
mybank  7
        +++ "CMS COMMAND MYBANK EXEC A1 mybank CMS"
    1 *-* /*-----------------------------------------------------------------//-
program to convert from one currency to another...    -//------------------
-----------------------------------*/
    4 *-* call initialize
   26 *-*  initialize:
        +++ Interactive trace.  TRACE OFF to end debug, ENTER to continue. ++
trace i  8
   27 *-*  'EXECIO * DISKR CURRENCY TABLE (STEM LINE.'
        >L>    "EXECIO * DISKR CURRENCY TABLE (STEM LINE."
say rc  9
0
say line.0  10
9

   28 *-*  do table_ct=1 to line.0
        >L>    "1"
        >L>    "LINE.0"
   28 +++  do table_ct=1 to line.0
    4 +++ call initialize
DMSREX476E Error 41 running MYBANK EXEC, line 28: Bad arithmetic conversion
Ready(20041);
```

Figure 36. MYBANK program—tracing at the Intermediates level.

Starting the program again (**7**), we can now set the tracing level to Intermediates by entering the REXX instruction TRACE I (**8**). As we progress from statement to statement by pressing Enter, we can see the breakdown of the statement, as REXX sees it. Now let's see some of the statements you can issue inside an interactive tracing session.

One of the things you can do is query the values of variables. In example part **9** , we are checking the value of the variable RC to ensure that the host command executed properly. We get a value of 0, which indicates that the EXECIO command worked. Now let's check out the value of the variable line.0 (**10**). We get a valid value, so we need to look further...

```
set exectrac on  11
Ready;
mybank
        +++ "CMS COMMAND MYBANK EXEC A1 mybank CMS"
    1 *-* /*----------------------------------------------------------//-
program to convert from one currency to another...    -//------------------
--------------------------------------*/
    4 *-* call initialize
   26 *-* initialize:
        +++ Interactive trace. TRACE OFF to end debug, ENTER to continue. ++
trace i
   27 *-* 'EXECIO * DISKR CURRENCY TABLE (STEM LINE.'
      >L>   "EXECIO * DISKR CURRENCY TABLE (STEM LINE."
say sourceline(28)  12
do table_ct=1 to line.0
do iii=28 to 30;say sourceline(iii);end  13
do table_ct=1 to line.0
   interpret line.table_ct
end
do iii=28 to 30;say iii sourceline(iii);end  14
   28 do table_ct=1 to line.0
   29    interpret line.table_ct
   30 end
exit  15
Ready;
```

Figure 37. MYBANK program—finding the cause of the problem.

Setting the external tracing on yet another time (**11**) may seem like a burden, but it's a lot better than leaving the TRACE instruction in the code.

After setting the tracing level to Intermediates, we can check out line 28 of the program using the SOURCELINE() function (**12**). This is the DO statement for our loop that interprets the currency table. We can incorporate a complete DO-loop (in a horizontal, one-line fashion), and this allows us to see the code for the loop (**13**). With the addition of the loop control variable in the SAY statement, we get not only the line, but also the line number (**14**). We can now see that the problem is the use of the letter O instead of the numeral 0 in the compound variable on the DO statement. This is what is causing the "Bad arithmetic conversion" error/message. Armed with this information, we can now exit the program (**15**), and go to edit the file and correct the program.

---

mybank   **1**
This program will allow you to convert any of the following
currencies to another. Please enter the amount:
25.00
The currency units are identified by the number in the list.
ENTER the FROM currency and the TO currency with a space between
(for example, 1 3 to convert from USA to POUNDs):
1 3
1. USA
2. YEN
3. POUND
4. MARK
5. FRANC
6. CANADIAN
7. LIRE
the value in POUNDs is 14.4217500   **2**
Ready;

Figure 38. MYBANK program—once it is corrected.

5.4 Trace Instruction—"Straight" versus Interactive

As can be seen from the MYBANK tracing, Interactive Debug
mode offers the whole world of REXX processing to the person
who wants to know more about the program that is executing. It
allows the modification of program variables as the program
progresses, thus causing the program to travel down different logic
paths during a given run of the program. This capability is one
that will be appreciated by those who test REXX programs for
correctness. In those environments where external setting of the
Interactive Debug mode is possible (for example, CMS), there is no
need to modify the program to add the TRACE instruction. Where
it is not available, some may opt to place a TRACE instruction
inside the program and make use of the TRACE VALUE
capability by specifying the trace option as an input argument
(and picking it up on the ARG template), thus allowing the
enabling of Interactive Debug by the way in which the program is
initiated. If the program you are working with is/was written for
an end user group, this may not be the best method for invoking
Interactive Debug mode—an end user might enter the TRACE
value setting on the command line accidentally, and when the

program runs, the TRACE output would be produced. This could (and most likely would) cause some concern on the part of the end user. The point is that having a "back door" may cause problems for the "innocent" end user who stumbles upon it.

In general, the choice of whether to use the TRACE instruction in "straight" or "interactive" is best made when taking these points into account (among others):

Familiarity How familiar are you with the workings of the program? If you are very familiar with the program from an internal processing point of view, then you may be satisfied with including the TRACE instruction in the section of the program that you feel needs to be explored. If you are not that familiar with how the program processes the data fed to it, you may want to use Interactive Debug to go through the program line by line or block of code by block of code. This will allow you to more clearly understand how the program is working (or not).

Time Using Interactive Debug will take more time than using the TRACE instruction in "straight" mode. Capturing the screen output into a file and then obtaining a printout of that file will be faster, but using Interactive Debug will allow the querying of program variables that have appeared earlier in the program, as well as the changing of the logic path(s) the program will follow during its run. In addition, the ability to issue host commands to "check things out" is very handy.

Access Do you have write access to the program you want to trace? If not, setting the Interactive Debug mode externally may be the only choice you have, for it will allow the tracing of the program once it is in primary storage, regardless of its origin disk/or library. No attempt is made to modify the copy of the program in secondary storage.

Chapter 6.
A Method for Debugging Your Program

There are two major kinds of errors that can occur with a program—a logic error, which can produce incorrect results, and a syntax error, which prevents normal execution of the program (a syntax error can be caused by a logic error as well as by improper coding techniques). The logic error is best found by placing SAY statements at various points in your program to track the values of variables, along with the use of the TRACE instruction (TRACE Labels would help pinpoint the origin of the incorrect processing). It requires knowledge of the programming logic as well as programming style. The syntax error can be found by using the following method.

1. Use the TRACE instruction to trace the Labels while the program executes. The last label displayed before the error occurs identifies the routine that contains the "culprit." This is your "target" label.

   Note: The use of interactive tracing is encouraged for this and all subsequent steps of this method.

2. Re-execute the program using the Labels level to TRACE until the target label appears. Once it appears, change the tracing level from Results to Intermediates.

65

3. Ensure that the proper arguments, if any, are being passed to the routine by tracing the ARG instruction.

4. Interactively trace the statements that follow the label.   If there are DO-loops that are "probably" not the cause (a judgment call here), use the numeric option of TRACE to process the loop without having to press Enter to step through the loop.

5. Once the "culprit" statement has been isolated, use the following section in this book to identify the more commonly found mistakes with that particular REXX instruction.   If the error statement is a host command, refer to the proper command manual that describes the syntax of the particular host command.

6. Fix the problem.

   Assumption: This method assumes that the error message(s) does not contain sufficient information to pinpoint the cause of the error.

Chapter 7.
Commonly Found Errors
(For Each Instruction)

7.1 ADDRESS Instruction

7.1.1 Background

The ADDRESS instruction is used to select the subcommand environment for any non-REXX statements in the program. There is a default subcommand environment for EXECs in each of the operating systems (i.e., for EXECs in CMS, the default environment is CMS, and the default environment for EXECs running in a TSO address space is TSO), and additional environments may also be available through REXX itself (i.e., an additional subcommand environment is available to EXECs in CMS; it is called COMMAND). Beyond the default environment that REXX provides, there are other environments that can be set up by other programs (i.e., the subcommand environment ISPEXEC is set up by ISPF in both the CMS and TSO environments).

When the ADDRESS instruction is used on the same line as a non-REXX statement, but not separated by a semicolon (';'), the specified subcommand environment will be used for that statement only. If the instruction is not followed by a non-REXX statement, the specified environment will be used for all non-REXX statements that follow (unless another ADDRESS instruction is encountered).

There is no limit to the number of times a subcommand environment may be chosen by using the ADDRESS instruction (of course, it is up to you to send the non-REXX statement to the proper place for processing). If you use the ADDRESS instruction as a complete statement (without either specifying an environment or supplying an expression), it is a "signal" to REXX to switch back to the last subcommand environment used. If you have the code in Fig. 39,

```
/* */
address 'DISPLAY'    (this becomes the active environment)

   ⋮
if RSTATUS = 'PF5'
   then
      do
         address 'COMMAND'  (now COMMAND is the active environment)
         'STATE PROFILE EXEC'

            ⋮

         address 'XEDIT'    (XEDIT is now the active environment)

            ⋮

         address            (switch back)

      ⋮
```

Figure 39. Using several ADDRESSes.

you will only be switching between the COMMAND and XEDIT subcommand environments. In other words, using ADDRESS as a complete statement will switch between the **currently active** environment and the **previously active** environment. In order to reactivate the DISPLAY environment, it would have to be explicitly stated on the ADDRESS instruction.

7.1.2 Examples

Here are some examples of commonly found errors using the
ADDRESS instruction:

```
/* */
userid= 'operator'
"state profile exec a"
if rc = 0
  then address command "msg" userid "yes, I have one"
  else address command "msg" userid "no, I don't have one"

   ⋮
```

This example contains two errors that are related to the
ADDRESS instruction. The first is that ADDRESS COMMAND
will not translate the non-REXX statement; this will cause a
mismatch with the MSG command (which has a name that
consists of upper-case letters). This can be fixed by having *all*
non-REXX statements be in upper case (refer back to Chapter 1
for a discussion of coding using upper or lower case). The second
problem is a bit more subtle. Along with not checking for
EXECS, the COMMAND environment also does not check for CP
commands. Since there is no CMS MSG command, the example
would still not run. To remedy this, any CP commands issued by
a REXX exec must be prefixed with "CP". If this is done, the
command will be passed to CP and executed. The corrected code
looks like this:

```
if rc = 0
  then address command "CP MSG" userid "yes, I have one"
  else address command "CP MSG" userid "no, I don't have one"

   ⋮
```

```
/*------------------------------------------------------------------*/
/* The address instruction in this example uses the subcommand      */
/* for the Display Management System (DMS/CMS).                      */
/*------------------------------------------------------------------*/
address 'DISPLAY'

   ⋮

if rstatus = 'PF6' then 'ERASE' fn ft 'A'

   ⋮
```

Figure 40. Using the wrong ADDRESS.

The error in Fig. 40 is caused by the use of the wrong subcommand environment. DMS/CMS requires the use of the DISPLAY environment for any of its commands that may appear as non-REXX statements in the exec. For this example, to issue the ERASE command (a CMS command) to CMS, do the following:

```
if rstatus = 'PF6' then address 'COMMAND' 'ERASE' fn ft 'A'
```

This will cause the ERASE command to be sent to the CMS environment (provided, of course, that the variable RSTATUS contains the string 'PF6'), but all remaining non-REXX statements will use the DISPLAY environment.

7.2 ARG Instruction

7.2.1 Background

The ARG instruction is used to pick up the arguments that were supplied to the EXEC or routine. The data from the arguments are translated to upper case (ARG is just a short form of PARSE UPPER ARG) and parsed into variables supplied on the template according to the rules of parsing (see "Advanced Parsing techniques" on page 41). The ARG instruction may be used more than once throughout the program (or routine); it will re-read the input parameter string each time.

The ARG instruction allows data to be *supplied* to the program or routine (but will *not* return any data). For information on how to return data from the program or routine, see the description of the SAY, EXIT, and RETURN instructions (in this chapter).

The majority of the problems encountered with the ARG instruction center around the use of commas. When commas are used in the template, REXX will look for the commas in the supplied argument string. These commas will then act as "mini-templates." If there are no commas in the supplied argument string, the complete argument string will be parsed into the argument(s) found before the first comma in the ARG statement.

Another mistake that is made when using the ARG statement concerns itself with the fact that ARG will convert input strings to upper case. This will cause problems if the EXEC is looking for lower-case arguments to be supplied.

7.2.2 Examples
Here are some examples of commonly found errors using the ARG instruction:

```
/* */
arg password rest
if password = 'hrdok'
  then say 'You made it!  Now you can continue...'
  else do
         say 'Wrong password - access denied'
         exit
       end

   :
```

This example will always fail, because ARG will convert the input string to upper case. When the comparison is made to the string 'hrdok', a match will not result because the strings are not in the same case. This can be remedied either by using PARSE ARG (which will not translate to upper case) or by changing 'hrdok' to upper case.

```
/*------------------------------------------------------------------*/
/* This example will calculate the surface area or volume of a  */
/* box; the user must supply dimensions of the box, as well as  */
/* a 'V' for Volume, or an 'A' for surface Area. For example,   */
/* an input string of "3 4 5 V" would yield a result of 60.     */
/*------------------------------------------------------------------*/
arg length width height choice
if choice = 'V' then call volume length width height
                else call area   length width height
say 'answer is = 'result
exit
/*--------------------------------*/
/* Volume subroutine             */
/*--------------------------------*/
volume: procedure
arg length, width, height
volume = length * width * height
return volume
/*--------------------------------*/
/* Area    subroutine            */
/*--------------------------------*/
area: procedure
arg length, width, height
area = (2*(length * width)) + (2*(length * height))
return area
```

The error in this example is caused by the use of the commas
inside the subroutines. All of the input values will be stored in
the variable LENGTH (including one blank between each pair of
numbers). This will be treated as a nonnumeric value and cannot
be used in an arithmetic expression. To remedy this problem,
either remove the commas from *both* of the ARG instructions (one
inside each subroutine) or use commas to separate the input
variables on the CALL instruction.

7.3 CALL Instruction

7.3.1 Background

The CALL instruction is used to invoke a routine; it may be an internal routine, a built-in function, or an external routine or program. Up to twenty expressions (also referred to as argument strings), separated by commas, may be supplied to the routine. The ARG instruction inside the routine that is being CALLed must have the same number of commas on its template in order to properly match each argument string to its corresponding "receptor" variables. Each argument string may have more than one value; this allows the passing of more than twenty arguments (values) to the routine. In addition, if no commas are used, the entire collection of arguments will be treated as one argument string (with a blank between each arguments' value). The ARG instruction should not use any commas when there are no commas used on the CALL instruction (and vice versa):

```
/*  */
a=2
b=3
d=4

  :

call int_routine a, b, d

  :

exit
int_routine:
arg g, h, i

  :

return
```

Figure 41. Calling a routine using commas.

```
/*  */
a=2
b=3
d=4

  :

call int_routine a b d

  :

exit
int_routine:
arg g h i

  :

return
```

Figure 42. Calling a routine without using commas.

Upon returning from a routine, the variable RESULT will contain any value or values returned; the variable will be set to an uninitialized state (DROPped) if the called routine does not return any values.

A subtle point about routines is the fact that REXX considers both subroutines and functions to be routines; this is very interesting when combined with the search order for routines:

1. Internal label that matches the routine name

2. Built-in function that matches the routine name

3. External EXEC (must be REXX) that matches the routine name

It is possible to CALL the built-in function DATE (yes, this means without using parentheses).   Instead of the value(s) returned from the routine being "substituted" into the statement, the value(s) will be placed in the variable RESULT, which can then be processed as any other variable.

One of the most commonly found mistakes when using the CALL instruction is the improper use of commas.   If the routine called uses commas in the template for the ARG or PARSE ARG instruction (for example, a function), then commas must be used in the CALL instruction to ensure that the data are "lined up" appropriately.

Another mistake that is made when using the CALL instruction is to attempt to CALL an EXEC that is written in EXEC 2 or CMS EXEC. When REXX CALLs an external routine, the external routine is assumed to be written in REXX (that is to say, the normal "what language is this EXEC written in" logic is not used).

7.3.2 Examples

Here is an example of one of the commonly found errors using the CALL instruction:

```
/*-----------------------------------------------------------------*/
/* This example will calculate the surface area or volume of a    */
/* box; the user must supply dimensions of the box, as well as    */
/* a 'V' for Volume, or an 'A' for surface Area. For example,     */
/* an input string of "3 4 5 V" would yield a result of 60.       */
/*-----------------------------------------------------------------*/
arg length width height choice
if choice = 'V' then call volume length width height
                else call area   length width height
say 'answer is = 'result
exit
/*--------------------------------*/
/* Volume subroutine             */
/*--------------------------------*/
volume: procedure
arg length, width, height
volume = length * width * height
return volume
/*--------------------------------*/
/* Area    subroutine            */
/*--------------------------------*/
area: procedure
arg length, width, height
area = (2*(length * width)) + (2*(length * height))
return area
```

The error in this example is caused by the mismatching of commas in the ARG instruction and the CALL instruction. All of the input values will be stored in the variable **length** (including one blank between each pair of numbers). This will be treated as a nonnumeric value (thanks to the blanks) and cannot be used in an arithmetic expression. To remedy this problem, either remove the commas from *both* of the ARG instructions (one inside each subroutine), or use commas to separate the expressions in the CALL instruction.

7.4 DO Instruction (DO ... END)

7.4.1 Background

The DO ... END structure (also called a DO group) is used to group statements together. This is useful when using IF or SELECT instructions; it provides for the association of a group of statements with a THEN or an ELSE. By default, a THEN or an ELSE (thing) will only execute one statement that immediately follows it. The DO group does not have to be completely on one line; it may cover several lines.

The most commonly found mistake using a DO group involves the use of the semicolon. If a statement is to follow a DO (on the same line), but is not a DO-loop, then a semicolon is required. Along the same line, if a statement is to follow an END (on the same line), a semicolon is required.

7.4.2 Examples

```
/* */
arg password rest
if password = 'hrdok'
  then say 'You made it!  Now you can continue...'
  else say 'Wrong password - access denied'
      exit

   .
   .
   .
```

This example will always fail, because the statement following the IF-THEN-ELSE is an exit. While it may be clear to the reader that the EXIT statement is meant to be executed only if the ELSE leg is taken, it is not treated that way by the interpreter. To remedy this, the IF_THEN_ELSE can be coded like this:

```
if password = 'HRDOK'
  then
    say 'You made it!  Now you can continue...'
  else
    do
      say 'Wrong password - access denied'
      exit
    end
```

7.5 DO Instruction (DO-Loops)

7.5.1 Background

There are many different kinds of loops made available in REXX. They provide for repetitive execution of a set of statements. The conditions controlling the execution of the loop are separated into two groups:

repetitors

       do forever

       do var = x to y by z

       do x (where x is a positive integer)

       do 5

conditionals

       do while x>y

       do until x>y

When combining repetitors and conditionals, only one of each may be specified on a DO.

Loops (in general)

The most commonly found mistakes using loops are as follows:

- Using SIGNAL to branch back into a loop after SIGNALing out of it. The SIGNAL instruction renders all currently active loops inactive; upon SIGNALing back into a loop, the return address that would normally be used when the END statement is reached would not be there, causing the program to ABEND. On the other hand, SIGNAL can be used safely from within a loop if the specified label is placed at or before the beginning of the outermost loop; this will cause the loop(s) to be initiated in a normal manner.

- Changing the value(s) of the variable(s) on the DO statement, causing the loop to terminate early, or in some cases not at all; also, some loops may "skip" values. This is not necessarily a mistake, unless it is unintentional.

- Using ITERATE instead of LEAVE (and vice versa); see the description of these instructions in this chapter.

- Using a DO WHILE (condition is checked *before* entering the loop each time) instead of DO UNTIL (condition is checked *after* executing the loop each time). Keep in mind that the DO UNTIL loop will always execute once, whereas the DO WHILE may not execute at all (both depend on the condition being tested).

- Not providing an exit from a DO FOREVER loop (the LEAVE instruction should be used). This will cause an endless loop (after all, you *did* instruct REXX to do it forever).

7.6 DROP Instruction

7.6.1 Background

The DROP instruction will return a variable to its uninitialized state. Compound symbols can be specified, in which case that particular compound symbol will be DROPped. If a stem is specified, then all storage associated with the compound variables with that stem will be freed. This puts all the compound variables in an uninitialized state (by being deleted from the variable table).

The most commonly found error with the DROP command lies in the misunderstanding of what is meant by "uninitialized" variables. A variable that is uninitialized contains its name (in upper case) as its value. For example,

---

DROP x score.1 score.2

---

will have the following effect:

- The variable x will contain "X"
- The variable score.1 will contain "SCORE.1"
- The variable score.2 will contain "SCORE.2"

Instead of specifying score.1, score.2, etc., the following can be used:

DROP score.

This will cause *all* compound symbols starting with score. to be dropped; score.7 will contain "SCORE.7", score.total will contain "SCORE.TOTAL", and so on.

Note: When using routines with PROCEDURE EXPOSE, ensure that the variables being DROPped within the routine are not associated with EXPOSE; doing so will change the values in the "calling" section.

7.7   EXIT Instruction

7.7.1   Background

The EXIT instruction will do just that; it will terminate execution of the program and return a whole number to the caller. The number can be explicitly listed, or it can be the result of the evaluation of an expression. If an expression is not given, no value will be passed back. If the program was called as an external routine from another REXX program, this will result in a syntax error.

The most commonly found error with the EXIT instruction is the attempt to have the EXIT instruction return more than one value. EXIT will return only one value, and it must be numeric; more specifically, it must lie in the range of -(2**31) to (2**31) - 1.

Another common error (related to EXIT) concerns itself with internal routines. It is a common practice to put internal routines at the "end" of the program's "main" section. To avoid falling into the first routine and executing the code (instead of normal termination of processing), place an EXIT instruction before the first routine, thus separating the main section from the routine section.

7.8   IF Instruction

7.8.1   Background

The IF instruction is used to conditionally execute a statement or group of statements. If a group of statements is to be executed, that group must be defined by a DO group (DO ... END). If a DO group is not used, the first (and only the first) statement that follows the THEN or ELSE will be executed. This may result in a drastic change in the intended flow of logic (especially if an EXIT statement is within that group of statements).

The IF instruction has three parts:

The if test The condition being tested

The THEN leg The action(s) to be taken if the if test is true (yields a '1').

The ELSE leg The action(s) to be taken if the if test is false (yields a '0').

The ELSE leg is optional; however, the THEN leg is required. Also, if the ELSE leg is to be on the same line as the THEN leg, the ELSE must be preceded by a semicolon.

Another aspect of the IF instruction is the creation of "null" legs (a null THEN or a null ELSE). To create a null leg, use the NOP instruction (which performs no operation). Don't use a semicolon; the semicolon is a clause delimiter, not an end-of-statement indicator.

```
/* */
arg input
if input = '?'
  then
    call help
  else
    nop
  ⋮
If input = '?' then call help;else nop
  ⋮
```

Figure 43. Horizontal and vertical IF-THEN-ELSE.

Note: The variable THEN cannot be used in an expression, for this will be picked up as a "keyword"; the expression being tested by the IF is bounded by the words IF and THEN.

7.9 INTERPRET Instruction

7.9.1 Background

The INTERPRET instruction is used to execute statements built (dynamically) by evaluating expression. Expression can consist of any instruction, but all instructions must be complete (i.e., DO ... END and SELECT ... END). The variables in expression are evaluated, and concatenated with any quoted strings. This "new statement" is then executed as if it were written into the program.

The most commonly found mistake using the INTERPRET instruction is the misuse of quotes in expression. If any literals are to be used in the "new statement," then both sets of quotes (single and double) should be used.

7.9.2 Examples

Here are some examples of commonly found errors using the INTERPRET instruction:

```
/*  this example reads in an arithmetic expression, and evaluates it */
arg expression
interpret 'say expression = expression'
```

This example will be evaluated as follows:

The entire character string will become the "new statement," which could be read as "SAY (the result of) EXPRESSION = EXPRESSION". The two variables will be compared for equality, and a "1" will be displayed, because the same variable is being compared to itself. This is not the desired result. The correct way is:

```
interpret 'say "expression ="' expression
```

The "new statement" created by this interpreted statement is

```
say expression "=" (whatever the value of expression is)
```

7.10   ITERATE Instruction

7.10.1   Background

The iterate instruction is used to "skip over" the remaining code inside a DO-loop. It can also be thought of as a "branch" to the END statement of a DO-loop. If a name is not specified, the innermost loop that contains the ITERATE instruction will be "skipped"; if a name *is* specified, the name is expected to be the name of the control variable of an active loop. The loop will continue processing as if the end statement was reached normally.

The majority of the problems encountered with the ITERATE instruction center around the use of the ITERATE instruction outside of a DO-loop, but within a DO ... END structure. This instruction was designed to work only in a DO-loop (a repetitive

structure).   If the DO ... END structure is contained within a
DO-loop, then the ITERATE instruction will "skip over" the code
until it reaches the END of the DO-loop.

Another mistake that is made when using the ITERATE
instruction is when the name that is specified does not match the
name of a control variable associated with an active loop (possibly
a nested loop). This occurs at times when a DO WHILE or a DO
UNTIL loop is specified, but without a loop control variable. If
you want to use ITERATE inside one of these loops, then add the
variable name to the DO statement, but do not supply a final
value (a beginning value must be specified).   You can then
"ignore" this control variable, and ITERATE will work as desired.

7.10.2 Examples

Here are some examples of commonly found errors using the
ITERATE instruction:

```
/* */
a=0
do while a < 5
    if a=3 then iterate a
    say a
end

    ⋮
```

This example will always fail because the variable **a** is not a
control variable; it is part of the WHILE condition. There are
two ways to correct this error—do not specify a variable name
after the ITERATE (which is no problem because there is no
nesting here), or change the DO statement to read   "DO I=1
while a < 5", and specify the variable I after the ITERATE.

7.11 LEAVE Instruction

7.11.1 Background

The ITERATE instruction is used to "terminate" the currently active DO-loop. It can also be thought of as a "branch" to the statement *after* the END statement of a DO-loop. If a name is not specified, the remaining code in the innermost loop (containing the LEAVE instruction) will be terminated; if a name *is* specified, the name is expected to be the name of the control variable of an active loop. The specified loop will terminate, and processing will continue with the statement following the END of the terminated loop.

   The majority of the problems encountered with the LEAVE instruction center around the use of the LEAVE instruction outside of a DO-loop, but within a DO ... END structure. This instruction was designed to work only in a DO-loop (a repetitive structure). If the DO ... END structure is contained within a DO-loop, then the LEAVE instruction will "terminate" the DO-loop (along with the remainder of the DO ... END group).

   Another mistake that is made when using the LEAVE instruction is when the name that is specified does not match the name of a control variable associated with an active loop (possibly a nested loop). This occurs at times when a DO WHILE or a DO UNTIL loop is specified, but without a loop control variable. If you want to use LEAVE inside one of these loops, then add the variable name to the DO statement, but do not supply a final value (a beginning value must be specified). You can then "ignore" this control variable, and LEAVE will work as desired.

7.11.2 Examples

Here are some examples of commonly found errors using the LEAVE instruction:

```
/* */
a=0
do while a < 5
   if a=3 then leave a
   say a
end

   ⋮
```

This example will always fail because the variable **a** is not a control variable; it is part of the WHILE condition. There are two ways to correct this error—do not specify a variable name after the LEAVE (which is no problem because there is no nesting here), or change the DO statement to read "DO I = 1 while a < 5", and specify the variable I after the LEAVE.

```
/* */
DO FOREVER

    ⋮
   do i = 1 to 10

      ⋮
      if ... then LEAVE

      ⋮
   end

    ⋮
end
```

The LEAVE in this example will exit the "DO I = 1 to 10" loop only, and the DO FOREVER loop will continue. When a LEAVE is issued without specifying a variable (i.e., LEAVE A), the loop that is affected is the innermost loop that contains the LEAVE instruction. If you want to LEAVE the DO FOREVER, there will have to be a LEAVE instruction that is contained inside the DO FOREVER loop, but outside any nested loops.

7.12   NOP Instruction

7.12.1   Background

The NOP instruction is a dummy instruction (it performs No OPeration). It is extremely useful for creating a "null" clause (for a THEN, ELSE, or OTHERWISE).

The major problem encountered with the NOP instruction centers around the lack of its use. Quite often, a semicolon is used after a THEN or an ELSE to create a "null" leg. This construct is supported in some other languages; however, REXX will just consider the semicolon to be the end of a clause, and will not treat it as a "null leg." To correct this, use the NOP instruction:

7.12.2   Examples

Here is an example of a commonly found error using the NOP instruction:

```
/* */
arg info .
fixit = ''
if info = 'fixit'
  then signal start
  else ;
a=2

   .
   .
   .
```

This example may not fail, but it could produce invalid results. The statement after the ELSE (a = 2) will be considered part of the ELSE branch (when the IF condition is true), and therefore will be skipped when the THEN branch is taken. This may cause problems later in the code. To correct this, change the "else ;" to read "else nop".

7.13 NUMERIC Instruction

7.13.1 Background

The NUMERIC instruction is used to control the precision (DIGITS), the form of exponential notation (FORM), and the number of digits that will be ignored during a comparison operation (FUZZ).

The major problem encountered with this instruction lies in its nonuse (the reliance upon the default setting for the number of significant digits) when **comparisons** are being made. The heart of the problem actually lies in the nonunderstanding of how comparisons are made in REXX.

First and foremost, the concept of all data being stored as strings (this means numbers also) has to be kept in mind. When comparing strings of data, REXX will first examine the data to see if they represent numbers only; if so, the numbers will be subtracted. This is where the setting of NUMERIC DIGITS will come into play.

7.14 OPTIONS Instruction

7.14.1 Background

The OPTIONS instruction was introduced with Release 4 of VM/SP. Its purpose is to notify REXX that Double-Byte Character Set functions are to be used in a particular exec. It is triggered by specifying a character string containing EXMODE or NOEXMODE. The last occurrence of either term is the one that REXX will honor. If EXMODE is specified, REXX will look at character strings differently; it will recognize the shift-in and shift-out characters when performing certain functions that deal with string manipulation. The functions in REXX that work with DBCS language strings are

DBCENTER()

DBRIGHT()

DBLEFT()

DBVALIDATE()

among others...

7.15　PARSE Instruction

7.15.1　Background

The PARSE instruction is an extremely complex instruction; at least it seems to be. However, even with so many forms in which it can exist, it has only one function—to retrieve data (from various sources) and assign them to one or more variables contained in the template. If no template is specified, then the retrieved data are ignored. If the UPPER option is specified, the data are translated to upper case before parsing occurs.

The PARSE instruction actually consists of three parts—the UPPER option (described in the preceding paragraph), the origin of the data, and the template that contains the variables that will store the data. The UPPER option is self-explanatory; the other two parts are not.

The origin of the data for each variant of PARSE is as follows:

Arg The information provided to the EXEC or routine, upon invocation.

```
EXEC myexec argument1 argument2...

CALL mysubroutine argument1,argument2,...

x= myfunction(argument1,argument2,...)
```

External The information stored in the Terminal Input Buffer (sometimes referred to as the Console Input Buffer). Data are stored in the Terminal Input Buffer when originally invoking the exec by "typing ahead" or using the CP TERM LINEND character to separate input lines. If the Terminal Input Buffer is empty, then the interpreter will read from the console.

Numeric The internal values currently in effect to control the options of the NUMERIC instruction (described earlier in this guide).

Pull The information stored in the Program Stack (sometimes referred to as the Console Stack). One line from the top (head) of the stack is removed, and made ready for parsing. If the Program Stack is empty, the Terminal Input Buffer is used. If the Terminal Input Buffer is empty, then the interpreter will attempt to read from the console.

Source The internal information describing the source of the EXEC being executed (how it was invoked, what its full name is, etc.).

Value The information that results from the evaluation of expression; WITH is used as a keyword to signify the end of expression.

Var The value of the variable name made ready for parsing; the name must be a valid variable name.

Version The internal information describing the level of REXX that is installed, and the interpreter release date.

The information available from ARG, SOURCE, and VERSION is static within a given routine; that is, the same information will be retrieved each time these options are used. The other options may change, based on program logic.

The template is a list of variable names and (optionally) patterns which control how the data will be stored into the variables. If only variable names are specified on the template, then the data are split up into "words" (blank-delimited character strings), and each word is assigned to a variable in sequence. Patterns are used with variable names to redefine the concept of a "word" (the data will not be separated just by blanks, but by position, or matching of literal patterns—these alternate methods are described in Part 5 of the SPI reference). If there are fewer words than there are variables on the template, all remaining variables are set to the null string (a string of length 0). If there are more words than there are variables, the last variable will get whatever is left or the original data, which could include both leading and trailing blanks (the last variable on a template is treated differently from the other variables). A period may be used to take the place of a variable at any point on the template. It is *not* a variable, and cannot be queried; it can, however, be the "recipient" of data.

The most commonly found mistakes when using the PARSE instruction center around the use of the template. At the top of the list is the problem with extra blanks in the variable that is the last one in the template. This can be remedied by using a period as a "dummy" variable.

```
/* */
say "enter your first and last name:"
pull response
/*---------------------------------------------------------------/
/-  let's assume "Molly Kiesel  " was typed in...              -/
/---------------------------------------------------------------*/
parse var response first last
/*---------------------------------------------------------------/
/-  the variable "first" contains "MOLLY"                      -/
/-  the variable "last"  contains "KIESEL    "                -/
/---------------------------------------------------------------*/
if last == 'KIESEL'
   then say 'Proceed'          /* does not display Proceed   */

   :

parse var response first last .
/*---------------------------------------------------------------/
/-  the variable "first" contains "MOLLY"                      -/
/-  the variable "last"  contains "KIESEL"                     -/
/---------------------------------------------------------------*/
if last == 'KIESEL'
   then say 'Proceed'          /* displays Proceed           */

   :
```

Figure 44. Parsing to avoid trailing blanks.

Another mistake that has been found is the use of literal and relative patterns. When a literal pattern is used in the template, it is removed from the string being parsed. However, when a literal string is used in conjunction with a relative position pattern, the literal string pattern becomes a "starting point," continuing for the length specified by the relative pattern. This combination of patterns behaves differently, depending on which release of REXX you are using (the action described here is using the Release 4 version of REXX in VM/CMS).

```
/*--------------------------------------------------------------/
/- Get the Social Security Number (SSN) from the data line  -/
/--------------------------------------------------------------*/
data_line='/REINHOLD, WW/AGE=31/SSN=123-45-6789/RANK=CAPTAIN/'
parse var data_line name_age '/SSN=' soc_sec_num +11 rank
/*--------------------------------------------------------------/
/- "name_age"    contains "/REINHOLD, WW/AGE=31/SSN="       -/
/- "soc_sec_num contains "/SSN=123-45"                      -/
/- "rank"        contains "-6789/RANK=CAPTAIN/"             -/
/--------------------------------------------------------------*/
```

$$\vdots$$

Figure 45. Parsing using a literal and relative pattern.

Other information on the effect of templates can be found in Section 4 of the SPI reference.

7.16 PROCEDURE Instruction

7.16.1 Background

The PROCEDURE instruction is used to protect existing variables from modification by an internal routine (subroutine or function). This can be modified (to allow certain variables to be modified) by using the EXPOSE option.

The majority of the problems encountered with the PROCEDURE instruction center around the use of the instruction in a routine that attempts to reference the values of the variables owned by the caller. If all variables are to be considered global, then the PROCEDURE instruction should not be used; simply reference the variables. By default, all variables are available to any routine unless the PROCEDURE instruction is encountered. Upon return from an internal routine, all variables (except those specified after an EXPOSE) will be restored to their value at the time before the invocation of the routine.

Note: When an external routine or EXEC is involved, all variables will be protected from modification by the external routine or EXEC.   The use of PROCEDURE EXPOSE will not override this.

   Another mistake that is often made is the attempt to pass a group of stemmed variables (sometimes referred to as a "stemmed array") to an internal routine on the CALL instruction, or within the parentheses on a function invocation.

```
/**/
names.1='Ian'
names.2='Bill'
names.3='Camille'
names.4='Jon'
names.5='Pete'
names.group='HRDOK'

   :

call int_routine names.

   :

exit
int_routine: PROCEDURE
arg quintet.
if quintet.2='Bill'
   then
      say 'The HRDOK quintet is complete;'
      say 'our 1st trumpet player came.'

   :

return
```

   This example will fail because **quintet.2** will contain the string "QUINTET.2", not "Bill".   To remedy this, the EXPOSE option should be used to make the stem **names** global to this routine.   In this case, **names.whatever** should be used in the routine.

```
int_routine: PROCEDURE EXPOSE NAMES.
if names.2='Bill'
  then
    say 'The HRDOK quintet is now complete;'
    say 'our 1st trumpet player came.'

    ⋮

return
```

7.17 PULL Instruction

7.17.1 Background

The PULL instruction is used to remove one line of data from the Program Stack and store it in the variable(s) listed on the template. If the stack is empty, the Terminal Input Buffer is used. If that is empty, the interpreter will read from the screen. If no template is specified, the data from the stack (or the screen) will be ignored.

The most commonly found mistakes when using the PULL instruction center around the use of the template. At the top of the list is the problem with extra blanks in the variable that is the last one in the template. This can be remedied by using a period as a "dummy" variable.

Another mistake that is made when using the PULL statement concerns itself with the fact that PULL will convert input strings to upper case. This will cause problems if the exec is looking for lower-case arguments to be supplied.

7.17.2 Examples

Here are some examples of commonly found errors using the PULL instruction:

```
/* */
say "enter the password to continue:"
pull password rest
if password = 'hrdok'
  then say 'You made it!  Now you can continue...'
  else do
        say 'Wrong password - access denied'
        exit
      end

  ⋮
```

This example will always fail, because PULL will convert the input string to upper case. When the comparison is made to the string 'hrdok', a match will not result because the strings are not in the same case. This can be remedied either by using PARSE PULL (which will not translate to upper case) or by changing 'hrdok' to upper case.

7.18 PUSH Instruction

7.18.1 Background

The PUSH instruction is used to "push" information onto the Program Stack in a last-in, first-out order. These data will remain on the Stack until a PULL is issued. The Stack can be subdivided by using the MAKEBUF and DROPBUF commands (covered in the CMS Command and Macro Reference for the VM environment, and the REXX Reference for the TSO and OS/2 environments). The number of lines currently in use on the Stack can be determined by using the QUEUED() built-in function. The number of lines represents *all* the lines on the Stack, not just those within a given buffer.

The majority of the problems encountered with the PUSH instruction center around the use of the PUSH as if it were a first-in, first-out instruction. Use QUEUE for this. When using the PUSH instruction, the data to be placed on the Stack must be in reverse order (the last line of data must be PUSHed onto the Stack first).

Another mistake that is made when using the PUSH instruction is the misuse of quotes. If a line of data is to contain quotes when it is placed on the Stack, then both types of quotes (single and double) must be used. The expression specified with the PUSH instruction is evaluated before the data are placed on the Stack; this removes one "level" of quotes. This is why both types of quotes are needed (see the section on quotes in Chap. 1).

7.19 QUEUE Instruction

7.19.1 Background

The QUEUE instruction is used to place information onto the Program Stack in a first-in, first-out order. These data will remain on the Stack until a PULL is issued. The Stack can be subdivided by using the MAKEBUF and DROPBUF commands (covered in the CMS Command and Macro Reference for the VM environment, and the REXX Reference for the TSO and OS/2 environments). The number of lines currently in use on the Stack can be determined by using the QUEUED() built-in function. The number of lines represents *all* the lines on the Stack, not just those within a given buffer.

The majority of the problems encountered with the QUEUE instruction center around the use of the QUEUE as if it were a last-in, first-out instruction. Use PUSH for this. When using the QUEUE instruction, the data to be placed on the Stack should be in logical order (the first line should be QUEUEd first).

Another mistake that is made when using the QUEUE instruction is the misuse of quotes. If a line of data is to contain quotes when it is placed on the Stack, then both types of quotes (single and double) must be used. The expression specified with the QUEUE instruction is evaluated before the data are placed on the Stack; this removes one "level" of quotes. This is why both types of quotes are needed (see the section on quotes in Chap. 1).

7.20 RETURN Instruction

7.20.1 Background

The RETURN instruction will do just that; it will return from a routine or EXEC, and optionally return a result to the point of its invocation.   If no internal routine is active, RETURN is essentially identical to EXIT (see the description of EXIT earlier in this chapter).

If the routine is invoked as a subroutine (via the CALL instruction), the data from expression will be placed in the variable RESULT upon RETURN (RESULT may be parsed to split the data into other variables); if expression is not specified, RESULT is DROPped.   If the routine is invoked as a function, expression *must* be specified; the data from expression will be used in the original statement at the point where the function was invoked.

7.21 SAY Instruction

7.21.1 Background

The SAY instruction is used to display information on the console. Expression can be any length.   SAY will display the information on the display without any formatting of the data; if the number of characters to be displayed is greater than the screen width, the information will "wrap around" to the next line on the display.

The most commonly found mistake using the SAY instruction is the misuse of quotes in expression.   If any literals are to be displayed, quotes should be used; anything not contained in quotes is considered to be a variable (except for numbers, which are allowed to be outside quotes).   If a variable is not found, it will be created as an uninitialized variable (it will contain its name in upper case as its value).

Note: This can cause unnecessary cycles for the interpreter, especially if there are many literals that should be inside quotes. To aid in identifying literals that should be inside quotes, SIGNAL on NOVALUE is available (this is further described in the SPI reference).

Another commonly found mistake when using the SAY instruction is the use of the HT (Halt Typing) command. The HT command will prevent the output of the SAY instruction from being displayed. This sometimes creates a very confusing environment when debugging REXX code; you may not be aware that certain messages and/or prompts are not being displayed (because of the HT command). HT can be "switched on" by using SET CMSTYPE HT (in CMS) or EXECUTIL HT (in TSO).

7.22 SELECT Instruction

7.22.1 Background

The SELECT instruction is used to conditionally execute one of several statements. Any expression that returns a Boolean value may be specified after a WHEN. If more than one statement is to be associated with a WHEN, a DO ... END construct is required. The OTHERWISE clause must be included if there is any chance that none of the WHEN clauses will return a value of 1 (true).

The majority of the problems encountered with the SELECT instruction center around the use of the END clause. Every DO used in the SELECT instruction must have a corresponding END. Beyond that, there must be an "additional" END clause to close out the SELECT statement itself. Failure to include this "additional" END may cause some of the statements following the SELECT to be considered part of an OTHERWISE clause (if the OTHERWISE keyword is specified). This could result in incorrect processing.

7.23 SIGNAL Instruction

7.23.1 Background

The SIGNAL instruction is used to branch to an internal label. The search for the label begins from the top of the file each time the SIGNAL instruction is encountered, unless a condition is specified; in that case, the search is triggered by an "external" event.   Once the label is reached, the variable SIGL will contain the line number of the statement that caused the branch.   The "external" events are further described in the REXX reference.

The majority of the problems encountered with the SIGNAL instruction center around the use of the SIGNAL instruction in the context of loops.   When a SIGNAL instruction is issued from the inside of a DO-loop, all active loops are terminated (the same applies to IF, SELECT, and INTERPRET instructions—they will be terminated also).   If a section of code is to be bypassed inside a DO-loop, the ITERATE, LEAVE, and IF instructions are available to accomplish this.

7.24   TRACE Instruction

For a description of the TRACE instruction, refer to Chap. 5.

7.25   UPPER Instruction

7.25.1   Background

The UPPER instruction is used to convert the contents of one or more variables to upper case.   Any number of variables may be specified.   The variables specified must be simple variables (the variable name may not contain a period), or compound variables. A stem of a compound variable may *not* be specified.

Chapter 8.
REXX Performance in VM

As mentioned earlier, REXX offers a great deal of flexibility to the programmer, in terms of programming style (coding style). A program can be written in many different ways; as long as the syntax is correct, REXX will allow almost any implementation of an algorithm. However, there are some areas of REXX coding where the programmer should consider the readability and maintainability of a program. This chapter will address some of these areas.

The areas that will be discussed are:

- How REXX issues CP/CMS commands
- Use of EXECLOAD/EXECMAP/EXECDROP
- Quotes around external routine calls
- How can I really "speed up" my program?

8.1 How REXX Issues CP/CMS Commands

There are two types of statements that can be found in a REXX program: REXX statements and non-REXX statements. A REXX statement begins with one of the following:

1. A label (a symbol of up to 249 characters, followed by a colon)
2. A symbol (variable), as in an assignment statement
3. A REXX instruction or a REXX comment line
4. Anything else (this is considered a non-REXX statement)

99

When REXX comes across a non-REXX statement, the statement is prepared to be sent to another processor (other than the interpreter) by evaluating any expressions that are not enclosed in quotes, and concatenating them with any character string (identified by use of quotes). The resultant string is then "tossed out the window" to the other processor or subcommand environment.

There are two "windows" (subcommand environments) provided by REXX: CMS and COMMAND. The default window is CMS. A statement that is passed through this window is treated as if it were entered on the command line in CMS. The statement is translated to upper case, and a search is made to attempt to discern what type of statement it is. (A list of these steps will be provided later.) The COMMAND window causes the statement to follow a slightly different path—the statement will *not* be translated to upper case, and it will not look for an EXEC that matches the first word of the string. Instead, it picks up at step 3 in the order that the CMS window uses. The benefit of this window (COMMAND) is twofold. First, two trips through the user's search order are saved; this could save considerable time if there are many minidisks accessed that contain large directories. Second, the readability of the program will be increased; the user must ensure that the command, upon resolution, is sent as a string of upper-case characters (unless the module/EXEC/routine name contains lower-case characters and/or can accept lower-case input). The easiest method for dealing with this situation is to place all nonvariable clauses of the non-REXX statement in upper case and use quotes to save the interpreter the trouble of looking in the variable table for values of something which is not a "real" variable. This method will cause the host commands (non-REXX statements) to stand out when you look at the code (if the rest of the program statements are in mixed or lower case). The increase in performance (you can expect a 3x increase in the execution of your EXEC), combined with the benefit of increased readability, makes this method a practical one.

8.2 Use of EXECLOAD/EXECMAP/EXECDROP

Each time an EXEC is invoked (from the command line, or from inside another EXEC), the EXEC is read from disk into storage, and executed.   If the disk that contains the EXEC is not ACCESSed, either the EXEC that tried to run that EXEC will not work (bad return code) or a different program that has the same name may be executed (which could produce some strange results).

There may be times that a disk containing some EXECs (that will be called later) will need to be released; it would be nice to have a way to get all of the EXECs in storage all at once, and run them from there.   To accomplish this, EXECLOAD, EXECDROP, and EXECMAP were introduced in VM/SP Release 4.

EXECLOAD will load a copy of the EXEC from disk into storage (the user has the choice of his/her own free storage or the nucleus free storage); this EXEC will remain in that section of free storage until an EXECDROP command is issued for that EXEC.   All of the necessary EXECs may be EXECLOADed into storage at any time (provided there is enough space).   EXECMAP will provide information about what EXECs have been loaded (and are still present) and how many times each was executed.

Allowing EXECs to remain in storage can help increase performance; each time an "external" EXEC is run, a new copy is read off disk.   This could also be a problem if the disk was released or if the EXEC was modified (intentionally or otherwise). These problems are bypassed when the EXECs are resident in storage.

8.3 Quotes Around External Routine Calls

Placing quotes around calls to "external" or built-in routines will cause the interpreter to not look in the file for a label that matches the referenced routine. This not only saves a few cycles (depending on the size of the program and the number of labels), but also allows the EXEC writer to use an internal label that matches the name of a function.

8.4 How Can I Really "Speed Up" My Program?

Here are some suggestions:

- Use ADDRESS COMMAND in your EXEC whenever you have non-REXX statements.   This will potentially avoid two trips through your search order, which could save considerable execution time.   Also, the COMMAND environment forces the use of the CMS command EXEC to execute another EXEC. This aids greatly in the readability of your EXEC, and also increases the maintainability of your EXEC.

- Be judicious about the use of PROCEDURE in internal routines; when the PROCEDURE instruction is encountered, REXX will start a new variable (symbol) table by saving the pointer to the caller's table and restoring the caller's table upon return.   If there are a large number of variables in the tables, there is a possibility of paging problems (in terms of time).   One of the main reasons behind the decision to use the PROCEDURE instruction is to "protect" variables from being altered by a called routine.   The additional discipline needed to avoid the use of PROCEDURE may well be worth the execution time saved.

- Use EXECLOAD if there are many external EXECs that will be run from the current EXEC.   As mentioned earlier, each time an EXEC is invoked, it is read from disk into storage.   If EXECLOAD is used, the file is read in once, and remains in storage until EXECDROP is issued for that EXEC.   This saves the time involved in reading the file from disk (which could be considerable, depending on the load on the system).

- Use quotes around nonvariable data; this saves the interpreter from having to look in the variables (symbol tree) for a value and/or adding a new entry (which really shouldn't be there). See "Quotes in REXX" in Chap. 1.

- Consider rewriting some of the highly repetitive "paths" of your EXEC in a compiled language;   as efficient as the REXX interpreter is, an interpreted language cannot compete with a compiled language. Balance this with maintainability.

- When reading a file, read it in all at once, if possible. If you are using Release 4 of VM/SP (or later), take advantage of the STEM option of the EXECIO command (found in the CMS Command and Macro Reference). If your system has Release 3 of VM/SP, the file may be read into the Program Stack and read into compound variables.

Part 3.
Editor Macros

Chapter 9.
Introduction

An editor macro is a program that is designed to interact with a specific command processing environment other than the operating system. An application is an example of such a command processing environment. A text editor is one such application. This chapter will focus on the text-editor command-processing-environment macro.

From time to time, you may have a need to do some "fancy stuff" when creating a document (or file or program). For example, you may need some information from another file. You could edit (or browse) that file, write down the needed information, and then input the results into the document you are creating. Or you could write a macro to do the work for you. As another example, you may need to perform some arithmetic on the contents of a certain file, and make some modifications accordingly. You could edit (or browse) the file, make the necessary calculations, and modify the file as needed. Or you could write a macro to do the work for you. If these activities are ongoing (that is, if they will have to be performed several times), then writing an editor macro can be just the thing you need to "free you up" to perform other tasks.

This chapter highlights the way REXX can be used to create editor macros. The XEDIT editor will be used to show examples. The concepts described here should apply to other editors.

Chapter 10.
What Are Editor Macros and Why Might I Want to Use One?

Editor macros are programs (which, in simplest form, could contain only editor commands) that are executed when the editor environment is active. These macro programs issue commands to the editor to make queries or modifications to a given file. REXX instructions can be used to assist in the control of the editor session. The main intent of allowing editor macros is to facilitate modifying files by allowing individuals to create their own programs to support their specific job needs.

A few years ago, someone approached me with the following question: "I know how to use the DELETE command to remove lines from a file when using XEDIT, but is there a way to delete certain columns from within a group of file records?"

This got me thinking about how a REXX program could be written to accomplish this task. REXX is not an editor. That meant that the editor itself would have to be used. After experimenting with several different methods of accomplishing this by hand, I came up with a sequence of steps that would work in an XEDIT session.[1]

Editor macros are used for a variety of reasons, but it all boils down to this—they are intended to make editing files easier for the person running the program. As you go through this chapter, you will see many examples of macro programs that offer a variety of ideas for programs that you can write. They require a knowledge of the editor and its capabilities, features, and functions, as well as a knowledge of the REXX language.

---

[1] I also became more familiar with the QQUIT command, which saved many a file from being altered because I was not using a "practice file."

Chapter 11.
How Do I Build an Editor Macro?

Once a sequence of steps was defined, it was time to put those steps into a REXX program. Since REXX allows the issuing of "host commands" to a subcommand environment, the XEDIT commands were easily made part of the REXX program.

11.1 Mechanics of Building an Editor Macro

The building (writing) of an editor macro is much the same as the writing of a REXX program (EXEC). The process of developing a program (gathering a clear understanding of the intended function, designing the algorithm to accomplish the desired function, and writing and testing the program) is assumed to be known; instead, this section will address the building of an editor macro from a REXX point of view.

The first point to be made is that the editor is its own subcommand environment, and will be the first environment in any chain that may exist for host commands. In the case of XEDIT, the default subcommand environment is the editor itself.

In other words, ADDRESS "XEDIT" could be placed in the beginning of the program, but it does not have to be put in the program at all. The host commands will go to XEDIT first, and XEDIT will control whether or not the statement goes elsewhere.

As with all host commands, it is recommended that the editor commands be written in upper case and their nonvariable parts be in quotes. Not only will this make the program easier to read and more efficient, but some editor commands are more sensitive to extra spaces, and could process the information in an unexpected way.

Usually, the filetype of an XEDIT macro is XEDIT. The filename should match the name of an editor command *only if* your intent is to *replace* the function of the editor's version of that command with your version. The XEDIT editor supplies some commands to help choose whether or not your version of a given command will be used or ignored. The filetype of the file does not have to be XEDIT, however. It can also be EXEC (just like any other REXX program in a CMS environment), and the editor commands inside will be issued to XEDIT. Be careful, though, for this version of a macro will work only if the editor environment is active at the time the program is executed.

An additional consideration when writing an editor macro is the way in which it will be invoked. There are three choices:

    The editor's command line
    The editor's Program Function (PF) key
    The editor's prefix area

The first two are nearly identical in the way input parameters are passed to the macro in that when the macro is invoked, the parameters are supplied after the macro name. The prefix area, however, can be a different story. The XEDIT editor supplies a rather unique input argument string to the macro invoked as a prefix macro. XEDIT provides the following arguments to a prefix macro:

```
PREFIX  SET|SHADOW|CLEAR  linenum  op1 op2 op3
```

where

PREFIX   is the indication that this macro was invoked from
              the prefix area.

SET|SHADOW|CLEAR is the indication that this macro was
              invoked on a displayed line, a shadow line,
              or if the macro was specified to replace a
              previously pending macro.

              Note: Only one value will be supplied.

linenum   is the line number of the file on which
              the macro was invoked.

op1 op2 op3   are the user-specified operands.

Figure 46. Argument string for XEDIT prefix macros.

Keeping this in mind when writing an editor macro can save
your macro some work if it is to be invoked from the prefix area
also. The first argument can be checked to see if it is the word
PREFIX; if so, the third argument is the line number on which
the macro was invoked. If not, then the arguments are all
user-supplied.

11.2 Helpful Commands for Building an Editor Macro

There are several commands available with editors. This chapter
will not address the use of all the commands; instead, here is a
list of the more commonly used commands when writing editor
macros:

ADD   Insert additional lines after the current line.

COUNT   Count the occurrences of a given string, and supply the
          response as a message.

CURSOR FILE Place the cursor in the file area upon exiting the
          macro.

CDELETE Remove characters from a file record, thus
          "shortening" the record. A column command.

CINSERT Insert characters at a given position in a file record, moving the remainder of the line over to "make room." A column command.

CLOCATE Move the "column pointer" to a specific character position; can be as a result of a search or an explicitly defined position. A column command.

COVERLAY Overlay certain fields in a file record. A column command.

CREPLACE Replace certain fields in a file record. A column command.

DELETE Delete the specified number of lines from the in-storage version of the file, starting with and including the current line.

EXTRACT /LASTMSG/ Capture the last message issued by the editor to make it available to the program. This will work even if SET MSGMODE OFF was issued.

EXTRACT /LINE/ Get the line number of the current line (relative to the file).

EXTRACT /CURLINE/ Get information about the current line, including the contents of the line in the file that is the current line.

FILE Exit the session, saving any file alterations.

INPUT Include a certain line of data immediately following the current line.

LOCATE Used to locate a certain character string; secondary use is as a GO TO (to get to a specific line number).

: (colon) Alternate form of the LOCATE command; used as a GO TO for a specific line number.

NEXT Move one line toward the end of the file.

QUIT Exit the session without saving any file alterations.

REPEAT Move the "line pointer" to the next line (towards the end of the file) and re-execute the previous command.

REPLACE Replace the contents of the current line with specified data.

SET CASE Controls the automatic conversion to upper case of the file.

SET LINEND Override the default line end character (used as a command separator) to allow the use of that character without "confusing" the editor.

SET MSGMODE Block messages from being displayed on the screen. Helps make the macro more "user friendly."

SET ZONE Restrict the columns to be searched by a LOCATE command.

TOP Make the top line of the file the current line. In other words, go to the top of the file.

Chapter 12.
Sample XEDIT Macros

This section will show examples of XEDIT macros that have been written to assist in "making the editor do a lot more work for you." The capabilities of editor macros are endless; this section focuses on three areas:

Text-processing macros

Text-modifying macros

XEDIT macros to help write REXX programs

Each example is followed by a discussion that points out certain aspects of the editor's capabilities that were used in that example. Subsequent examples build on some of the ideas and techniques used in previous examples.

12.1 Text-Processing Macros

As mentioned previously, there are several uses for editor macros. This section will focus on examples of text-processing capabilities where the editor can be told to "read" a file and report back to the calling program with information on the file. This allows the REXX program writer to take advantage of the searching capabilities, among others, of the editor. Why write a program to perform a particular function when the editor can do it for you?

The first of these, COUNTEM XEDIT, demonstrates this principle. The next example, TOTALEM EXEC, demonstrates a method that can be used to look at a file containing a list of numbers, and return their sum. A second version of TOTALEM will show how the sum can then be inserted into the file following the list of numbers.

Author's note: Each example carries with it an implied assumption (on the part of the macro writer) that specific information is known about the file the macro is to process. There is no "magic" here.

12.1.1   Editor Macro—COUNTEM XEDIT

This macro is going to show how we can make use of some of the actual editor commands to "do some of the work for us" in trying to determine the number of occurrences of a given string in a file (or section thereof). There are several ways this program (or any program, for that matter) can be written. This is one of the shorter methods.

```
/*----------------------------------------------------------------/
/- This macro will count the occurrences of a single search -/
/- string. The zone to be searched can be specified also.  -/
/- The number of occurrences will be returned as the return -/
/- code. The input values are expected to be on the stack,  -/
/- in the following order (brackets denote optional items): -/
/- "zone_beg zone_end" search_string                        -/
/----------------------------------------------------------*/
address 'XEDIT'              /* send all host commands to XEDIT */
'SET MSGMODE OFF'    1               /* don't display messages */
pull zone_beg zone_end search_arg .  2
if zone_end = ''
   then search_arg = zone_beg       /* only a search_arg was  */
   else                             /* entered                */
     do
       'SET ZONE' zone_beg zone_end /* search requested zone  */
     end
```

Figure 47 (Part 1 of 2). COUNTEM XEDIT—count occurrences of a string.

```
/*----------------------------------------------------------------/
/- Issue the count against the file, and capture the message -/
/----------------------------------------------------------------*/
'SET CASE MIXED IGNORE'     3
'COUNT /'search_arg'/ *'    4
'EXTRACT /LASTMSG/'         5
'SET MSGMODE ON'            6
parse var lastmsg.1 msgno number .    7
if datatype(number,'N') =1    8         /* search_arg found      */
  then
    do
      'COMMAND QUIT 'number         /* use number as "RC"    */
      exit number
    end
'COMMAND QUIT 0'              /* not found           */
exit 0
```

Figure 47 (Part 2 of 2). COUNTEM XEDIT—count occurrences of a string.

Let's now take a look at the parts of COUNTEM XEDIT.

As with most[2] REXX programs, the first line of the program must start with the beginning-of-a-REXX-comment characters (/*). The first executable statement of this macro is the ADDRESS instruction, which designates the XEDIT subcommand environment as the host command environment for all non-REXX statements.

The REXX PULL instruction (2) is used to obtain the search argument as well as the settings for the search zone. If only one argument is passed to the macro, it is assumed to be the search string, and each record is to be searched (the full length of the record). If only a portion of each record is to be searched, the beginning and end of the zone can be specified along with the search argument.

---

[2] The exception is when a REXX program is to be used as an external subroutine or function from another REXX program. In this case, REXX assumes that the EXEC contains REXX code, and the initial comment line is not required. This applies only to a file with a filetype of EXEC.

The macro processing centers itself around the XEDIT COUNT command (**4**) which will count the occurrences of a specified string of characters while searching a specified number of lines. The XEDIT current line is of importance, since the COUNT command starts with that line of the file; when the macro is used in "batch" mode (that is, when it is executed from within a program and not from within the editor itself), the first line of the file can be thought of as being the current line. The COUNT command returns its information in the form of an XEDIT message, hardly the form that one would want to have in order to use the command in a REXX program. Communicating with a user in this manner is fine, but we are using a program, not a person. This poses quite a dilemma.

XEDIT provides another command to assist with this dilemma—the EXTRACT /LASTMSG/ command (**5**). This command allows the program to "ask" XEDIT to get the last message it just issued, and place it in the variable **lastmsg.1** (**7**), which can then be used by the macro. Knowing the message format is essential to making best use of the EXTRACT command. In this case, the second word of the message is the number of occurrences; if there are no occurrences, then the second word is "No."

Putting this together, we can make use of the DATATYPE built-in function (**8**) that is provided in REXX to determine whether the second word of the message is numeric or not. If it is, that number is used as the return code for the macro. If it is not numeric, then a zero (0) is used as the return code.

The XEDIT SET MSGMODE OFF command (**1**) is used to prevent the message from the COUNT command from being displayed on the screen; this allows more control of output messages generated by the macro. It is turned back on with the SET MSGMODE ON command (**6**) once it is "safe" to do so (after the last XEDIT command that would produce an output message).

The last XEDIT command covered here is the SET CASE MIXED IGNORE command (**3**). Its purpose is to allow "HOUSE", "house", "House", etc., to be recognized as matching the search argument "HOUSE". Of course, if the macro is to be less tolerant of case, then SET CASE MIXED RESPECT can be used. This will cause a match only when the strings are identical.

12.1.2 Editor Macro—TOTALEM XEDIT

This macro wants to add up a list of numbers that are in a file such that each number is on a different line. Each number may have a dollar sign preceding it. The editor does not allow any arithmetic such as the kind the program needs, so all we can do is "grab" each line that has a number, get the number into a REXX variable, and let REXX do the arithmetic. We are making use of the editor commands to "grab" the lines from the file.

```
/*---------------------------------------------------------------/
/-  This macro will locate a list of numbers in a file and     -/
/-  return their sum.  The list of numbers is preceded in      -/
/-  the file by a line of asterisks ('*') and followed by a    -/
/-  line of equal signs ('=').  The numbers are not always     -/
/-  in the same columns in each record, but are always the     -/
/-  fourth word of each record. There may or may not be a      -/
/-  currency sign with each number (in this case, the dollar   -/
/-  sign will be used).  Valid numbers will be assumed for     -/
/-  this example.                                              -/
/---------------------------------------------------------------*/
address XEDIT              /* send all host commands to XEDIT */
currency='$'
sum=0
'LOCATE /***************/'  1     /* find start of numbers list */
'EXTRACT /LINE'            2
start = line.1 + 1        3      /* point to line after '*'s    */
'LOCATE /===============/'        /* find end   of numbers list */
'EXTRACT /LINE'
end   = line.1 - 1               /* point to line before '='s  */
do line = start to end
    'LOCATE :'line        4
    'EXTRACT /CURLINE'    5                  /* get each line     */
    parse var curline.3 . . . number .  6a /* parse out number */
    number = strip(number,'L',currency) 6b
    sum=sum + number                   6c
end
push sum                  7          /* make sum available */
'COMMAND QUIT'            8           /* leave XEDIT session*/
```

Figure 48. TOTALEM XEDIT—add a list of numbers.

Let's now take a look at the parts of TOTALEM XEDIT.

The adding of the numbers (**6b** through **6c**) is no mystery; let's focus on the use of the XEDIT commands.   The EXTRACT /LINE/ command (**2**) allows the macro writer to make use of the work performed by the LOCATE command (**1**) The LOCATE command, in essence, says, "find this string, and make that line of the file the current line."   The EXTRACT /LINE/ command (**2**) says "tell me the line number of the current line."   This value is returned in the variable **line.1** (**3**).   The list of numbers to be processed begins at the line *after* the one represented by **line.1** when LOCATEing the start string, and ends at the line *before* the one represented by **line.1** when LOCATEing the end string.

The second use of the LOCATE command (4) takes advantage of the "GO TO" function provided by the LOCATE command. When a "target" consisting of a colon (:) and a number is used, the command performs a "go to this line and make it the current line" function. The EXTRACT /CURLINE/ command (5) is used to bring the *contents* of the current line into the macro (remember that the EXTRACT /LINE/ command was used just to get the line number of the current line). The variable **curline.3** (6a) contains the actual contents from the line, and the data can then be parsed to isolate the desired number.

Once the sum is calculated, the value is placed on the stack (7), which enables the calling program to have access to its value. The COMMAND QUIT (8) is used to leave the XEDIT session without having to resave the file. The file is not being altered in this example, but it is always safe to use COMMAND QUIT to avoid requiring user interaction. If the file is to be altered by the macro, then SAVE or FILE (or an equivalent) might be necessary.

12.1.3 Editor Macro—TOTALEM XEDIT

This version of the TOTALEM macro differs in how the total is handled:

```
/*-----------------------------------------------------------------/
/-  This macro will locate a list of numbers in a file and   -/
/-  insert their sum.  The list of numbers is preceded in    -/
/-  the file by a line of asterisks ('*') and followed by a  -/
/-  line of equal signs ('=').  The numbers are not always   -/
/-  in the same columns in each record, but are always the   -/
/-  fourth word of each record. There may or may not be a    -/
/-  currency sign with each number (in this case, the dollar -/
/-  sign will be used).  Valid numbers will be assumed for   -/
/-  this example. A line containing "Total:" followed by the -/
/-  sum will be inserted before the ending line of '='s.     -/
/-----------------------------------------------------------------*/
address 'XEDIT'            /* send all host commands to XEDIT */
currency='$'
sum=0
'LOCATE /***************/'    /* find start of numbers list */
'EXTRACT /LINE'
start = line.1 + 1           /* point to line after '*'s   */
'LOCATE /==============/'     /* find end  of numbers list */
'EXTRACT /LINE'
end   = line.1 - 1           /* point to line before '='s  */
do line = start to end
   'LOCATE :'line
   'EXTRACT /CURLINE'                    /* get each line      */
   parse var curline.3 . . . number .  /* parse out number   */
   number = strip(number,'L',currency)
   sum=sum + number
end
push sum/* make sum available */
'COMMAND INPUT Total:' sum        1      /* insert into file   */
'COMMAND FILE'                    2      /* leave XEDIT session*/
```

Figure 49. TOTALEM XEDIT—a slightly different version.

Let's now take a look at how this version differs from the previous one.

Instead of the sum being made available only to the calling program by being placed on the stack, it is inserted into the file by use of the INPUT command (**1**). The line pointer is positioned such that the last line containing a number is now the current line. The INPUT command places the specified characters at a line immediately following the current line, and "pushes" the rest of the lines in the file down by one (in other words, it "makes room" for the new line). The other difference in this version is the use of the FILE command (**2**). Since the INPUT command alters the file, the FILE command (or an equivalent) must be used if the alteration is to be made permanent. This goes one step further than looking at the data inside a file and processing them; it actually modifies the file, which leads us into the next part of this chapter—text-modifying macros.

12.2 Text-Modifying Macros

The previous section of this chapter showed some examples of macros that will look at the contents of a file and perform some processing, returning the data to the calling program. Now let's look at how macros can be used to actually alter the document or file on which we are working.

Who might be interested in this particular section? Anyone who:

- Creates documents (i.e., SCRIPT files, order blanks, form letters, etc.)

- Creates programs (written in almost any programming language—REXX, Pascal, FORTRAN, COBOL, LISP, C, etc.)

- Creates files that follow a particular format (i.e., data files)

We will begin by looking at some small but particularly helpful macros that have helped several people over the years—COLDEL, COLINS, COLOVER, COLREP, and FT. Following those, we will look at some that have been helpful to many people when writing REXX programs. Again, the XEDIT editor commands are used in the macros.

12.2.1 Editor Macro—COLDEL XEDIT

Back in 1984, a friend approached me with the following question:

I know how to delete one record from a file, and I know how to delete a block of records from a file. How can I delete some columns from a block of records in XEDIT?

I thought about it, and realized I would need to do some digging to find out how to do this. After a bit of reading the manual, I came across the CDELETE command, which would delete a specified number of columns from *one* record in a file. This was close, but not quite what was needed. Still more digging uncovered the REPEAT command, and the combination of the two started me off in the right direction.

```
/*----------------------------------------------------------------/
/- This XEDIT macro will delete columns in a file, given a  -/
/- starting column number and an ending column number       -/
/- (inclusive), followed by the number of consecutive lines -/
/- from which the columns are to be deleted. An asterisk     -/
/- ('*') may be substituted for the number if ALL records    -/
/- in the file (from the current line) are to have the       -/
/- columns deleted.                                          -/
/------------------------------------------------------------*/
arg startcol endcol how_many_records .
Address XEDIT
'CLOCATE :'startcol        1
length = (endcol-startcol) +1
'CDELETE 'length           2
'REPEAT 'how_many_records  3
'TOP'   4
```

Figure 50. COLDEL XEDIT—remove specified columns from a file.

Let's now take a look at COLDEL.

This program makes use of three XEDIT commands to do its work. The two commands that set things up and perform the first delete are CLOCATE and CDELETE (which can be thought of as "column locate" and "column delete"). The REPEAT command does just that; it repeats the last XEDIT command after moving to the next line in the file until the end of the file is reached.

The CLOCATE command (1) moves what can be thought of as a "column pointer" to the specified column position. For those editors that provide a scale showing character positions in a record, the effect of this should be quite clear. The "family" of column-pointer-dependent commands will act on the record starting at the character position pointed to by the column pointer.

The CDELETE command (**2**) will delete the specified number of characters from the record, and *will shorten the* record (see COLREP for an example of how to "blank out" a field in a record). The "family" of column-pointer-dependent commands will act on the record starting at the character position pointed to by the column pointer.

By the time the REPEAT command (**3**) is reached, the CDELETE command will already have been executed. The REPEAT command will move the line pointer to the next line in the file, and will re-execute the CDELETE command. When it reaches the number of lines that was specified, or the end of the file if an asterisk was specified, the command will terminate, and the file will be positioned such that line 0 is the current line.[3]

The TOP command (**4**) is used to reposition the file so that you see the file from its beginning.

12.2.2 Editor Macro—COLINS XEDIT

Once I saw that COLDEL met my friend's need, I started "getting into" writing XEDIT macros. In my discovering CDELETE, I also found CINSERT, which will *insert* a string of characters into the record. Thus began the creation of COLINS XEDIT.

---

[3] These macros start working with the current line, which may be any line in the file, including line zero (line 0, sometimes referred to as the top-of-file line). In this case, the column command will be effected on line 0, which could generate a "No line(s) changed" or similar message. Therefore, the number of lines on which the column command could be effected might be one less than specified. However, the REPEAT command will move to the next line (which would now be line 1) and re-execute the command.

In other words, if the file was positioned with line 0 being the current line, which could be accomplished by issuing the TOP command on the command line, and

```
COLDEL 5 10 4   (delete columns 5 through 10 on the next 4 lines)
```

was specified, then lines 1 through 4 would have columns 5 through 10 removed. In reality, five CDELETEs were executed; the first was "spent" on line zero.

```
/*--------------------------------------------------------------/
/-  This XEDIT macro will insert a given character string in -/
/-  records of the file at a certain column, moving the      -/
/-  original characters over a few positions (based on the   -/
/-  length of the character string). The parameters are the  -/
/-  starting column, the number of records, and the string.  -/
/--------------------------------------------------------------*/
arg startcol how_many_records string  1
address XEDIT
'CLOCATE :'startcol
if string='' then string=' '
'CINSERT 'STRING  2
'REPEAT 'how_many_records
'TOP'
```

Figure 51. COLINS XEDIT—insert a specified string into file records.

Let's now take a look at COLINS.

Admittedly, this program looks very similar to COLDEL, but its function is the exact opposite from the function of COLDEL. Instead of removing characters and shortening a record, it adds characters and lengthens the record.   Because the string is specified as an input argument to the program, the order of the parameters (**1**) is a bit different from the order used in COLDEL.

Again, the issue of how many CINSERTs are actually executed comes into play. The REPEAT command (**2**) helps us out again. One execution of the CINSERT command will be spent on whatever line happens to be the current line.   The number of times the command is executed will be one more than the number specified when this macro is invoked.   Of course, one way to remedy this is to see whether the current line is also the top-of-file line, and if so, to move ahead one line and repeat the command up to the specified number of records minus one.

One caveat when using the CINSERT command in XEDIT is that it may cause the line to SPILL onto the next line; this can happen just as easily as it can happen when inserting characters in a line on a terminal display.

12.2.3 Editor Macro—COLOVER XEDIT

Not being satisfied with just having COLDEL and COLINS, I decided to go ahead and write another macro that would "sort of" insert a string into a file record, but this time I decided to use the COVERLAY command that XEDIT provides. This will not lengthen the record, but there is an interesting behavior with the COVERLAY; this behavior is described in the program comment (yes, that's right—a comment; at times they come in handy).

```
/*----------------------------------------------------------------/
/- This XEDIT macro will overlay records in a file with a    -/
/- specified string of characters.  If the specified string -/
/- contains any blanks, characters in those position will   -/
/- NOT be overlaid.  If you want to place a blank in a       -/
/- certain character position, use the '_' (underscore) in   -/
/- the specified string (one for each blank).  The '*'       -/
/- (asterisk) character can be used to overlay fields in ALL-/
/- records from the current line to the end of the file.     -/
/----------------------------------------------------------------*/
arg startcol how_many_records string
address XEDIT
if string='REXX COMMENT' 1
  then string='/*'||copies(' ',61-(startcol+1))||'*/'
'CL :'startcol
'COVERLAY 'string
if datatype(how_many_records,'N') 2
  then how_many_records=how_many_records-1
'REPEAT 'how_many_records
'TOP'
```

Figure 52. COLOVER XEDIT—overlay a specified field in file records.

Let's now take a look at COLOVER.

This program has some additional functions that COLDEL and COLINS do not have. The first is the recognition of the string **REXX COMMENT** (**1**). The second is the checking of the datatype() of the variable **how_many_records**. These will be discussed in reverse order.

The use of the DATATYPE() (**2**) built-in function is one answer to the question "how many times will the COVERLAY command actually be executed?"   In this program, the fact that the COVERLAY command is executed one extra time is compensated for.   Note the subtraction of 1 from **how_many_records** to compensate.   If the datatype of the variable is not numeric, it is assumed to be an "*", and passed to the REPEAT command.

The reassigning of the variable **string** is to provide a function that could come in handy for those who program in REXX.   It allows one to take a program that is already written and place some uniform comments on the right-hand side, along with the code. While there is bound to be some difference of opinion on whether this is a "good" coding practice or not, it shows how some XEDIT functions can be used for creating files or documents. The common right-hand edge of the comments makes for easier reading.   The calculating of the number of blanks in the comment takes the starting column into account.

12.2.4   Editor Macro—COLREP XEDIT

In order to "round out" my collection of COLxxxx macros, I came up with one to use the COLREP command.   Again, the comment box describes the action this command takes when blanks are included in the string you specify.

```
/*-------------------------------------------------------------/
/- This XEDIT macro will replace records in a file with a   -/
/- specified string of characters. If the specified string -/
/- contains any blanks, characters in those position WILL   -/
/- be replaced. The '*' (asterisk) character can be used to -/
/- replace fields in ALL records from the current line to   -/
/- the end of the file.                                     -/
/-------------------------------------------------------------*/
arg startcol how_many_records string
address  XEDIT
if string='REXX COMMENT'
  then string='/*'||copies(' ',61-(startcol+1))||'*/'
'CL :'startcol
'CREPLACE 'string
if datatype(how_many_records,'N')
  then how_many_records=how_many_records-1
'REPEAT 'how_many_records
'TOP'
```

Figure 53. COLREP XEDIT—replace a specified field in file records.

Let's now take a look at COLREP.

Admittedly, this program is identical to COLOVER, with the exception that all characters in the specified field will be replaced with the string provided to the macro. Again, in the case of a REXX COMMENT argument being passed to the macro, there will be a common right border for the comments.

Author's note: Don't worry; the next macro is completely different.

12.2.5   Editor Macro—FT XEDIT

This is another text-modifying macro that can come in handy when looking at files in XEDIT. After a few rounds of splitting and joining lines, a block of text can start to look a bit ragged. The idea behind this macro is to read in each line, up to a predetermined stop point (it could be a blank line, or a colon (:) in column 1; you decide). As the lines are read in, they are concatenated into one long string. Then, word by word, the string is shortened (from the beginning), and the length is checked to see if it still fits into the specified length. Once a line is built that "just fits" into the specified length, it is stored in a compound variable. This continues until the large string is exhausted of its values. The new lines are written out to the file, and the old lines are deleted from the file. After this is completed, the file is displayed.

```
/*---------------------------------------------------------------/
/- Name          -  FT      XEDIT                          -/
/- This macro will format the text within a paragraph in a  -/
/- given file.  The test will be left-justified within a    -/
/- field of 70 columns (can be overridden by specifying the -/
/- right hand margin after FT).  If a colon, slash, period,  -/
/- or a string of 25 blanks is found in column 1, that will  -/
/- be considered the end of the paragraph.                   -/
/---------------------------------------------------------------*/
address 'XEDIT'
'SET LINEND OFF'
arg prefix .
if prefix='PREFIX'
  then arg . . prefline maxlinelength
  else arg maxlinelength
if maxlinelength=''
  then maxlinelength=70
'COMMAND EXTRACT /LINE'
'COMMAND EXTRACT /CURSOR'
if cursor.3<=0 then exit 100
if cursor.4<=0 then cursor.4 = 1
if prefix¬='PREFIX'
  then line=cursor.3
  else line=prefline
'COMMAND :'line
/*---------------------------------------------------------------/
/-  read in the lines to be formatted                      -/
/---------------------------------------------------------------*/
text=''
```

Figure 54 (Part 1 of 4). FT XEDIT—format text in a paragraph.

```
do n=0 by 1
   'COMMAND EXTRACT /CURLINE'
   if rc¬=0 then leave
   if i¬=1 then
     do
       if substr(curline.3,1,25) = copies(' ',25) then leave
       if substr(curline.3,1,1)='.' then leave
       if substr(curline.3,1,1)=':' then leave
       if substr(curline.3,1,1)='/' then leave
     end
   text=text strip(curline.3)
   'COMMAND NEXT'
end
'COMMAND UP'
if i = 1 then exit /* only one line was to be formatted */
```

Figure 54 (Part 2 of 4). FT XEDIT—format text in a paragraph.

```
/*--------------------------------------------------------------/
/- format the input lines - parse string by string until the -/
/- end has been reached (word will be equal to '' when this  -/
/- occurs).  Add the proper number of spaces following the   -/
/- punctuation characters.  If there is not enough room for  -/
/- a word on one line, move it down to the next.             -/
/--------------------------------------------------------------*/
i=1
lineo.=copies(' ',cursor.4-1)
do forever
   parse var text word text
   if word='' then leave
   if length(lineo.i) = cursor.4-1
     then
       do
          lineo.i = lineo.i||word
          iterate
       end
   punctuation=substr(lineo.i,length(lineo.i))
   if punctuation¬='.' & ,
      punctuation¬='?' & ,
      punctuation¬='!' & ,
      punctuation¬=':'
     then lineo.i=lineo.i' '
     else lineo.i=lineo.i'  '
   if length(lineo.i||word)>maxlinelength
     then i=i+1
   lineo.i=lineo.i||word
end
no=i
/*--------write the formatted lines to the file--------------*/
'COMMAND ADD' no
do i=1 to no
   'COMMAND NEXT'
   'COMMAND REPLACE' lineo.i
end
```

Figure 54 (Part 3 of 4). FT XEDIT—format text in a paragraph.

```
/*--------go back and delete the original lines--------------*/
'COMMAND :'line
'COMMAND DELETE' n
'COMMAND :'line.1
'SET LINEND ON'
if cursor.4<=1
    then 'COMMAND CURSOR FILE' cursor.3 1 'PRIORITY 255'
    else 'COMMAND CURSOR FILE' cursor.3 cursor.4 'PRIORITY 255'
```

Figure 54 (Part 4 of 4). FT XEDIT—format text in a paragraph.

Let's now take a look at FT.

This macro makes use of a different set of XEDIT commands. The Cxxxxxx commands, which act on a specified character position, were helpful in the previous COLxxxx macros, but they will not help us with this one.

This macro is designed primarily to be run from the prefix area.[4] The last line in the prologue comment box shows what pieces of information XEDIT will pass to the macro upon invocation. If the macro is run from the prefix area, the first argument passed in is the string PREFIX. The second argument is not of importance in this example. The third argument is the line number on which the prefix macro was invoked. The fourth argument is the right margin column. If not specified, the default is column 70.

The 'COMMAND :'line command is similar to the LOCATE : command mentioned earlier in the discussion of TOTALEM XEDIT.

---

[4] It can be run from the command line, but because it only works on one "block" of lines, it is best run from the prefix area. This way, you can enter it on the starting line of more than one paragraph. Each occurrence will be a separate invocation of the macro.

12.3 XEDIT Macros to Help Write REXX Programs

The last examples in this chapter are some that have helped many people write REXX programs.   They are RCS, RCM, RDO, RIF, and RSEL. They are prefix macros that produce a REXX comment (single, RCS; multiline, RCM), a DO-END group at the proper indentation level (RDO), an IF-THEN-ELSE instruction at the proper indentation level (RIF), and a SELECT statement (RSEL). The indentation scheme will follow the one described in Chap. 1.

12.3.1 Editor Macro—RCS XEDIT

```
/*---------------------------------------------------------------/
/- REXX XEDIT macro to input a single-line comment at the    -/
/- proper level of indentation, and place the cursor in      -/
/- the comment for convenience.                              -/
/-----------------------------------------------------------*/
/*---------------------------------------------------------------/
/- get cursor position...                                    -/
/-----------------------------------------------------------*/
'EXTRACT /CURSOR'
startlin = cursor.3
/*---------------------------------------------------------------/
/- get line number of current line... will be restored.     -/
/-----------------------------------------------------------*/
'EXTRACT /LINE'
home = line.1
```

Figure 55 (Part 1 of 2). RCS   XEDIT—insert   a   single   REXX comment, properly indented.

```
/*--------------------------------------------------------------/
/- get contents of start line... here's where indenting    -/
/- level is determined.                                     -/
/--------------------------------------------------------------*/
'COMMAND :'startlin
'EXTRACT /CURLINE'
line=curline.3
parse var line firstone secondone .
first=firstone;upper first
select
  when first = 'IF'         then increment=2
  when first = 'DO'         then increment=2
  when first = 'THEN'       then increment=1
  when first = 'WHEN'       then increment=2
  when first = 'ELSE'       then increment=2
  when first = 'SELECT'     then increment=2
  when first = 'OTHERWISE'  then increment=2
  otherwise
    increment=0
end
startpos=pos(firstone,line) + increment
if startpos=1
  then startpos=0
  else startpos=max(startpos-1,0)
comment = copies(' ',startpos)||'/*'||copies(' ',59 - startpos)||'*/'
':'startlin
'INPUT' comment
':'home
'CURSOR FILE 'startlin+1 startpos + 5 ' PRIORITY 255'
```

Figure 55 (Part 2 of 2). RCS   XEDIT—insert   a   single   REXX
comment, properly indented.

Let's now take a look at RCS.

This program looks very much like the RC XEDIT program, but
the method of calculating the starting position is different. Instead
of relying on the cursor position to determine the indentation
level, the line on which the macro was entered is examined to see

if the line begins with one of the types of instructions that are generally used to determine indentation levels in a program.[5]

Once the cursor position has been determined, the line from the file is examined. The variable **first** is used to facilitate the process of checking to see if it is one of the recognized "keywords" listed in the SELECT statement. This will help choose the indentation increment that will be used along with the number of leading blanks to determine the starting point. Then we are ready to start inputting the comment into the file and then finally placing the cursor inside the comment.

There is a problem, however. You may have even noticed it if you tried some of the earlier examples of editor macros in this book. It is possible to enter a macro in the "prefix" area but leave the cursor on a different line of the file. In this case, relying on the cursor position is not always the best method. The next example, RCM XEDIT, shows another way of determining the line on which the editor macro was entered.

12.3.2 Editor Macro—RCM XEDIT

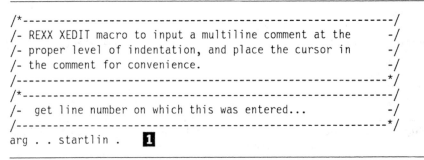

```
/*---------------------------------------------------------------/
/- REXX XEDIT macro to input a multiline comment at the      -/
/- proper level of indentation, and place the cursor in      -/
/- the comment for convenience.                              -/
/---------------------------------------------------------------*/
/*---------------------------------------------------------------/
/- get line number on which this was entered...              -/
/---------------------------------------------------------------*/
arg . . startlin .     1
```

Figure 56 (Part 1 of 2). RCM XEDIT—insert a REXX multiline comment, properly indented.

---

[5] The   END   statement   is   not   included   in   the   list   of indentation-level-determining   instructions;   the   code   needed   to determine   to   what   the   END   belongs   is   too   involved   for   these examples.

```
/*----------------------------------------------------------------/
/-  get line number of current line... will be restored.    -/
/----------------------------------------------------------------*/
'EXTRACT /LINE'
home = line.1
/*----------------------------------------------------------------/
/-  get contents of start line... here's where indenting    -/
/-  level is determined.                                     -/
/----------------------------------------------------------------*/
'COMMAND :'startlin
'EXTRACT /CURLINE'
line=curline.3
parse var line firstone secondone .
first=firstone;upper first
select
   when first = 'IF'        then increment=2
   when first = 'DO'        then increment=2
   when first = 'THEN'      then increment=1
   when first = 'WHEN'      then increment=2
   when first = 'ELSE'      then increment=2
   when first = 'SELECT'    then increment=2
   when first = 'OTHERWISE' then increment=2
   otherwise
      increment=0
end
startpos=pos(firstone,line) + increment
if startpos=1
   then startpos=0
   else startpos=max(startpos-1,0)
begin   = copies(' ',startpos)||'/*'||copies('-',59 - startpos)||'-/'
fill    = copies(' ',startpos)||'/-'||copies(' ',59 - startpos)||'-/'
end     = copies(' ',startpos)||'/-'||copies('-',59 - startpos)||'*/'
':'startlin
'INPUT' begin
'INPUT' fill
'INPUT' end
':'home
'CURSOR FILE 'startlin+2 startpos + 5 ' PRIORITY 255'
```

Figure 56 (Part 2 of 2). RCM XEDIT—insert a REXX multiline comment, properly indented.

Let's now take a look at RCM.

The difference here is found in the first instruction used in this program.   The ARG instruction (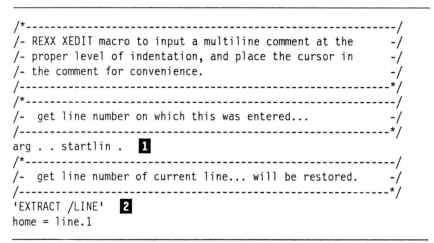) is being used to take advantage of the parameters passed to the program by the editor. The third piece of information passed to the macro is the line on which the macro was entered.   Using this instead of the cursor position not only allows the cursor to be left on a different line, but allows many macros to be entered on several lines.   When each macro is executed in turn, the editor will pass in the line number (on which that particular macro was entered) to each macro. With this technique, more work can be done per pressing of the Enter key.

These last two examples are for comments, and have used column 63 as a "wall" that is not to be crossed when INPUTting lines into the file.   This is, of course, based on the coding techniques discussed in Chapter 1 of this book.   Your program may make use of any available column position for the "wall" for comments.   The last three examples are not concerned with comments, and there will be a noticeable lack of the column 63 motif in determining the length of the line to be INPUTted into the file.

12.3.3 Editor Macro—RDO XEDIT

```
/*----------------------------------------------------------------/
/- REXX XEDIT macro to input a multiline comment at the      -/
/- proper level of indentation, and place the cursor in      -/
/- the comment for convenience.                              -/
/----------------------------------------------------------------*/
/*----------------------------------------------------------------/
/-  get line number on which this was entered...             -/
/----------------------------------------------------------------*/
arg . . startlin .
/*----------------------------------------------------------------/
/-  get line number of current line... will be restored.     -/
/----------------------------------------------------------------*/
'EXTRACT /LINE'
home = line.1
```

Figure 57 (Part 1 of 2). RDO XEDIT—insert a REXX DO group, properly indented.

```
/*---------------------------------------------------------------/
/- get contents of start line... here's where indenting     -/
/- level is determined.                                     -/
/---------------------------------------------------------------*/
'COMMAND :'startlin    4
'EXTRACT /CURLINE'     6
line=curline.3
parse var line firstone secondone .  7
first=firstone;upper first
select    8
  when first = 'IF'        then increment=2
  when first = 'DO'        then increment=2
  when first = 'THEN'      then increment=1
  when first = 'WHEN'      then increment=2
  when first = 'ELSE'      then increment=2
  when first = 'SELECT'    then increment=2
  when first = 'OTHERWISE' then increment=2
  otherwise
     increment=0
end
startpos=pos(firstone,line) + increment
if startpos=1
  then startpos=0
  else startpos=max(startpos-1,0)
doline  = copies(' ',startpos)||'do'
fill    = copies(' ',startpos)||' /*place statements here*/'
endline = copies(' ',startpos)||'end'

':'startlin         5
'INPUT' doline      5
'INPUT' fill        5
'INPUT' endline     5

':'home    3
'CURSOR FILE 'startlin+2 startpos+3 ' PRIORITY 255'
```

Figure 57 (Part 2 of 2). RDO XEDIT—insert a REXX DO group, properly indented.

Let's now take a look at RDO.

This macro is to be run as a prefix macro; that is, it is to be executed from the prefix area. This allows the program writer to determine where a REXX DO...END (a DO group) should be placed. The ARG instruction (**1**) is used to receive the line on which the macro was invoked; see Fig. 46 on page 113 for a description of the input argument string provided by XEDIT.

The 'EXTRACT /LINE' command (**2**) is used to capture the line number of the current line; the editor will place that number in the variable **line.1** (this macro takes that value and places it in the variable **home**), which can then be used later in the program (**3**) to set the current line back to the original line number when the macro was invoked. The ':'startlin and the 'INPUT' commands (**4** and **5**) changed the current line in order to position the DO...END correctly. By making use of the value in **home**, the macro can reposition the current line on exit, thus giving the appearance that a change was made to the file at a point other than the current line.

The 'EXTRACT /CURLINE' command (**6**) sets the stage for the indenting level. The line itself is copied into the variable **line** to facilitate the parsing of the line to examine its first word (**7**). The SELECT statement (**8**) can be thought of as "based on what the first word is on this line, I want to indent **x** number of spaces when the DO...END skeleton is inserted into the file."[6]

The actual indenting is carried out by finding where the first word is, from a character position point of view, then creating input lines that have the correct number of spaces to match the desired indenting level.

The last line of the macro places the cursor at the beginning of the line within the DO...END so that the appropriate statement(s) can be written without having to move the cursor to that position. This is just another little "extra" that can be added to macros to "help the program be more helpful" to the REXX macro writer.

---

[6] The values chosen for the variable **increment** reflect the author's coding style; any values may be entered to match your coding style.

12.3.4 Editor Macro—RIF XEDIT

```
/*----------------------------------------------------------------/
/- REXX XEDIT macro to input a multiline comment at the       -/
/- proper level of indentation, and place the cursor in       -/
/- the comment for convenience.                               -/
/-----------------------------------------------------------*/
/*----------------------------------------------------------------/
/-  get line number on which this was entered...              -/
/-----------------------------------------------------------*/
arg . . startlin .
/*----------------------------------------------------------------/
/-  get line number of current line... will be restored.     -/
/-----------------------------------------------------------*/
'EXTRACT /LINE'
home = line.1
/*----------------------------------------------------------------/
/-  get contents of start line... here's where indenting     -/
/-  level is determined.                                      -/
/-----------------------------------------------------------*/
'COMMAND :'startlin
'EXTRACT /CURLINE'
line=curline.3
parse var line firstone secondone .
first=firstone;upper first
select
  when first = 'IF'         then increment=2
  when first = 'DO'         then increment=2
  when first = 'THEN'       then increment=1
  when first = 'WHEN'       then increment=2
  when first = 'ELSE'       then increment=2
  when first = 'SELECT'     then increment=2
  when first = 'OTHERWISE'  then increment=2
  otherwise
    increment=0
end
startpos=pos(firstone,line) + increment
if startpos=1
  then startpos=0
  else startpos=max(startpos-1,0)
```

Figure 58 (Part 1 of 2). RIF   XEDIT—insert   a   REXX
IF-THEN-ELSE, properly indented.

```
ifline  = copies(' ',startpos)||'if'
thenline= copies(' ',startpos)||' then'
elseline= copies(' ',startpos)||' else'
':'startlin
'INPUT' ifline
'INPUT' thenline
'INPUT' elseline
':'home
'CURSOR FILE 'startlin+1 startpos+4 ' PRIORITY 255'
```

Figure 58 (Part 2 of 2). RIF   XEDIT—insert   a   REXX
IF-THEN-ELSE, properly indented.

Let's now take a look at RIF.

This macro is to be run as a prefix macro; that is, it is to be executed from the prefix area. This allows the program writer to determine where a REXX IF-THEN-ELSE statement should be placed. The ARG instruction is used to receive the line on which the macro was invoked; see Fig. 46 on page 115 for a description of the input argument string provided by XEDIT.

The 'EXTRACT /LINE' command is used to capture the line number of the current line; the editor will place that number in the variable **line.1** (this macro takes that value and places it in the variable **home**), which can then be used later in the program to set the current line back to the original line number when the macro was invoked. The ':'startlin and the 'INPUT' commands changed the current line in order to position the IF-THEN-ELSE instruction correctly. By making use of the value in **home**, the macro can reposition the current line on exit, thus giving the appearance that a change was made to the file at a point other than the current line.

The 'EXTRACT /CURLINE' command sets the stage for the indenting level. The line itself is copied into the variable **line** to facilitate the parsing of the line to examine its first word. The SELECT statement can be thought of as "based on what the first word is on this line, I want to indent **x** number of spaces when the IF-THEN-ELSE skeleton is inserted into the file."[7]

The actual indenting is carried out by finding where the first word is, from a character position point of view, then creating input lines that have the correct number of spaces to match the desired indenting level.

The last line of the macro places the cursor after the IF so that the IF condition can be written without having to move the cursor to that position. This is just another little "extra" that can be added to macros to "help the program be more helpful" to the REXX macro writer.

12.3.5 Editor Macro—RSEL XEDIT

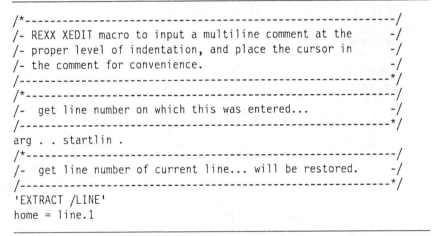

```
/*-----------------------------------------------------------/
/- REXX XEDIT macro to input a multiline comment at the     -/
/- proper level of indentation, and place the cursor in     -/
/- the comment for convenience.                             -/
/-----------------------------------------------------------*/
/*-----------------------------------------------------------/
/-  get line number on which this was entered...            -/
/-----------------------------------------------------------*/
arg . . startlin .
/*-----------------------------------------------------------/
/-  get line number of current line... will be restored.    -/
/-----------------------------------------------------------*/
'EXTRACT /LINE'
home = line.1
```

Figure 59 (Part 1 of 3). RSEL XEDIT—insert a REXX SELECT statement, properly indented.

---

[7] The values chosen for the variable **increment** reflect the author's coding style; any values may be entered to match your coding style.

```
/*-------------------------------------------------------------/
/- get contents of start line... here's where indenting   -/
/- level is determined.                                    -/
/-------------------------------------------------------------*/
'COMMAND :'startlin
'EXTRACT /CURLINE'
line=curline.3
parse var line firstone secondone .
first=firstone;upper first
select
  when first = 'IF'        then increment=2
  when first = 'DO'        then increment=2
  when first = 'THEN'      then increment=1
  when first = 'WHEN'      then increment=2
  when first = 'ELSE'      then increment=2
  when first = 'SELECT'    then increment=2
  when first = 'OTHERWISE' then increment=2
  otherwise
    increment=0
end
startpos=pos(firstone,line) + increment
if startpos=1
  then startpos=0
  else startpos=max(startpos-1,0)
```

Figure 59 (Part 2 of 3). RSEL XEDIT—insert a REXX SELECT
statement, properly indented.

```
selline = copies(' ',startpos)||'select'
whenline= copies(' ',startpos)||' when              then'
othwline= copies(' ',startpos)||' otherwise'
endline = copies(' ',startpos)||'end  '
':'startlin
'INPUT' selline
'INPUT' whenline
'INPUT' othwline
'INPUT' endline
':'home
'CURSOR FILE 'startlin+2 startpos+8 ' PRIORITY 255'
```

Figure 59 (Part 3 of 3). RSEL XEDIT—insert a REXX SELECT
statement, properly indented.

Let's now take a look at RIF.

This macro is to be run as a prefix macro; that is, it is to be executed from the prefix area. This allows the program writer to determine where a REXX SELECT statement should be placed. The ARG instruction is used to receive the line on which the macro was invoked; see Fig. 46 on page 115 for a description of the input argument string provided by XEDIT.

The 'EXTRACT /LINE' command is used to capture the line number of the current line; the editor will place that number in the variable **line.1** (this macro takes that value and places it in the variable **home**), which can then be used later in the program to set the current line back to the original line number when the macro was invoked. The ':'startlin and the 'INPUT' commands changed the current line in order to position the SELECT instruction correctly. By making use of the value in **home**, the macro can reposition the current line on exit, thus giving the appearance that a change was made to the file at a point other than the current line.

The 'EXTRACT /CURLINE' command sets the stage for the indenting level. The line itself is copied into the variable **line** to facilitate the parsing of the line to examine its first word. The SELECT statement can be thought of as "based on what the first word is on this line, I want to indent **x** number of spaces when the SELECT skeleton is inserted into the file."[8]

The actual indenting is carried out by finding where the first word is, from a character position point of view, then creating input lines that have the correct number of spaces to match the desired indenting level.

The last line of the macro places the cursor after the first WHEN in the SELECT skeleton that was just inserted into the file without having to move the cursor to that position. This is just another little "extra" that can be added to macros to "help the program be more helpful" to the REXX macro writer.

---

[8] The values chosen for the variable **increment** reflect the author's coding style; any values may be entered to match your coding style.

12.3.6   Chapter Summary

There are several uses for editor macros, ranging from the modifying of information in a file to assisting in program development.   The examples in this chapter used the XEDIT editor.   The editor you use may provide similar functions.   To begin writing editor macros, it is important to become familiar with the features of the editor you are using.   There is no magic in the writing of editor macros, but it can appear as such once a macro is written.   The ideas presented in this chapter do not constitute an exhaustive list of the features available in any editor; instead, they constitute some of the more commonly used features when writing editor macros.

Part 4.
User-to-Program
Interface Issues

Chapter 13.
Introduction

When learning a spoken language, once you learn what the "pieces" or basic vocabulary items are, the next step is to see how some of these pieces fit together. This applies also to learning a programming language. In this chapter, examples are provided to show how REXX can be used to produce some of the more common program "pieces" you are likely to need when writing REXX programs. For example, you might be looking for a way to handle input arguments (or input parameters) to a REXX program. Or, you might be looking for a way to "standardize" the code used to read/write files from within a REXX program. Another question might address the storing of REXX programs on your system, be it a mainframe system, a personal computer, or something in between.

Note: In this chapter, the discussions regarding input arguments are presented as being supplied by a user. The same issues apply to invoking a program from within another program.

The questions that are addressed in this section are:

- How can my program handle input arguments? How about default values?

- How can I read/write files?

- When can I use the SELECT statement instead of nested IF statements?

- How about setting up tables from a data file?

- How about presenting sparsely populated tables on the screen?

- How can I check for an available address?

- Do I always have to stack the response from a CP command?

- Is there any way to make a REXX "include" file?   What are the limitations?

- How can I store my REXX programs?

This chapter highlights examples of REXX program segments that address the above questions.

Chapter 14.
Handling Input Arguments

As you write your REXX programs, there are times when you want to identify all values for your program variables, and there are times when you want the values to be supplied when the program is run. There are two views on this subject. If you provide all values for your variables while you are writing the program, it will be easier to ensure proper execution by facilitating the testing of your program. With all the values already in the program, the need for sections of the program to provide data checking will not be necessary.

On the other hand, if you build your program in such a way that certain variables' values are provided by the user, then the program becomes more general-purpose, and thus you avoid the need for several versions of the program. The fewer versions of a program that are sitting around, the better. In addition, users will only have to remember one program name.

If you decide to let the users provide some of the values for program variables, you have to decide the point at which your program will accept those values. These values that are supplied to the program are called arguments.

14.1 When to Obtain Arguments

14.1.1 Deciding When to Accept the Arguments

A program can be thought of as being in one of two states, running or not running. The action that causes a program to change from a state of not running to a state of running can be thought of as *invoking a program*. You can supply the values at the time you invoke the program, or you can invoke the program and wait for it to ask you for the input arguments. To look at it another way, try Figs. 60 and 61.

Scenario: A parent wants to enroll a child in the day care program at The Little Red Schoolhouse. Miss Mary Beth answers the phone.

Parent: Do you have room for my child in your program?

Miss MB: That all depends; how old is your child?

Parent: 2 years old.

Miss MB: How often during the week would your child attend?

Parent: 2 days, Tuesday and Thursday.

Miss MB: Would your child be attending half or whole days?

Parent: Half days.

Miss MB: I think there is room in our program...

Figure 60. Invoke program, and wait for it to prompt.

Parent: Do you have room for my child in your program? My
child is 2 years old, would be coming on Tuesdays
and Thursdays, and would come for the mornings.

Miss MB: I think we have room in the program.

Figure 61. Invoke program, and supply all inputs at the start.

The point being made here with this example is that Miss Mary Beth would have to ask each question, wait for the response (which could be delayed if the 2-year-old was acting up while the parent was answering the questions), process the request, and deliver a response. If the parent supplied all the necessary information at the beginning of the phone call, the length of the call could have been shortened, and more requests could be handled in a smaller period of time.

Of course, the parent would have to know what information to supply. The user-program interface is the same way. If a user supplies all the information at the beginning when the program is invoked, the program can go off and "do its own thing," without having to wait at some point in its processing to get a response from the user.

The cost of this method of application design is the education of the user group. Depending on the "people" skills of the program writer(s), this may not be an easy task. A decision has to be made on the method of input of program arguments.

14.1.2 When the Program Is Invoked

Once you have decided that the input arguments are to be supplied at the time the program is invoked, you can look at REXX to see how this can be done. There are two instructions that can help you—ARG and PARSE ARG. Both are actually the PARSE instruction itself; it's just available in abbreviated form as ARG. The difference between the two is that ARG will take the input arguments and convert the alphabetic characters to their upper-case form. PARSE ARG will leave the input arguments as they were typed in. Quite often, when input arguments are processed, they are compared to some literal values in order to ensure correctness. Comparisons in REXX are made, in some cases, with padding of blank characters to "even things out"; however, there will never be a case where 'a' is equal to 'A'. The decision on whether to use ARG or PARSE ARG is crucial when comparisons are to be made with literal strings.

Caution: If you are running a REXX program in the ISPF/PDF editor environment, be sure you precede the program invocation with TSO if it is not an editor macro; if it is an editor macro, invoke it from the command line without preceding it with TSO.

Both instructions make use of a *template*. The template is a list of variables and, perhaps, some control strings. Every variable that appears in a template will receive a value, unless it is enclosed by a set of parentheses. Variables in the template are filled with values, starting with the (physically) leftmost variable in the template. If there are more input values than variables in the template, the last variable will receive the remainder of the input argument string, *including* any blanks found in the last part of the input argument string.   This also includes any trailing blanks at the end of the string, if the user types in some trailing blanks (for example, to correct a typo). Any variables that do not receive values from input arguments will be assigned the null string (" or ""). The null string is a string that has a length of zero.   The normal (default) way to divide up the input argument values is to separate them by blank characters.   The *input argument string*, which is what the complete set of input argument values is referred to as, is taken as a set of individual "words" that are separated by blank characters, and each *word* is placed into each variable that is listed in the template.

The   ideal   situation   is   one   in   which   the   number   of blank-delimited words in the input argument string matches the number of variables in the template. This is not always the case; in cases where there are "not enough input values to go around," the variables in the template that do not receive an input argument value receive, instead, something called the *null string*. This null string can be thought of as *empty*. It is a string with a length of zero.   It is nothing.   In some programming languages, the concept of *nothing* does not exist.   At the very least, a variable will hold as its value whatever happened to be at that storage location at the time the variable was established (created). The idea that a variable can be assigned nothing seems to conflict with that view. Instead of it conflicting with that view, consider that it is just another view (after all, some languages will place a blank character or a zero as an initial value).

To check to see if a variable is empty (in other words, to see if it has been assigned the null string), use the following construct:

```
if var = ''
```

The two single quotes (or apostrophes, if you prefer), placed alongside each other with *no* (repeat, *no*) spaces in between, denote the null string. If you were to check the length of the contents of a variable (using the length() routine), you would get a value of 0 as the result if the variable was empty (had been assigned the null string). Instead of two single quotes, you can use two double quotes (or two quotes, if you prefer); REXX doesn't care.

In addition to the concept of a variable in a template becoming empty, a template can consist of any combination of the following:

- Synchronization strings
- Numbers
- Variables in parentheses
- The period (.)

14.1.2.1 Synchronization strings

When looking at the input argument string, there may be times when you need to have the user supply information in the form *keyword* = *value* in order to "help keep things straight." In this case, the template can look like this: *ARG kwd* ' = ' *kwdval*. This causes the template to "line up" or "synchronize" itself at the ' = ', thus giving two *mini-templates*. The input argument string can be looked at as being split into two separate groups, and the values that go into the variables would be the input argument string (without the ' = '). In the basic template (no numbers used in the template), the synchronization string is not used as values for the template variables. Its purpose here is to split up the template into mini-templates. This rule applies unless there is a signed number following the synchronization string. See Sec. 14.1.2.2, "Numbers in the template—unsigned," for an explanation.

There can be any number of mini-templates; keep in mind that the practical limit is controlled by the length of the input argument string that can be supplied by the user.

The synchronization string can be more than one character in length. It does not make sense to have the string be of greater length than the input argument string itself, however.

14.1.2.2 Numbers in the template—unsigned

In addition to having a synchronization string in a template for the (PARSE) ARG instruction, numbers are allowed. They direct REXX by identifying where the variables' fields start in the input argument string. For example,

```
ARG 1 abc 10 def 15 ghi
```

will cause REXX to put the characters in columns 1 – 9 (inclusive) in the variable **abc**, the characters from columns 10 – 14 (inclusive) in the variable **def**, and the rest of the values into the last variable on the template (columns 15 to the end). A slightly different way of looking at this template is to read it as

The field for abc starts in column 1; the field for def starts in column 10; the field for ghi starts in column 15.

There is an implied '1' at the beginning of the template when column numbers are used.

There can be more than one variable between the column position numbers. In this case, the template is effectively split into mini-templates, and the normal rules of parsing apply (split by blanks, start from the left, the last variable in that *mini*-template receives all the rest of the values, etc.). In addition, synchronization strings can be used in the template along with column position numbers. Thus, you can have several mini-templates, based on how you want to split the data.

A not-so-obvious use of numbers in a template is the ability to take a "second pass" over the data. For example,

```
ARG fn ft fm 1 first_char 2
```

will take the data items and parse them into fn, ft, and fm, *then* go back to column a and place the character in column 1 into the variable *first_char*. If the column position numbers were not used, then a second statement (either another ARG or a substr() call, etc.) would be necessary. The ability to "go back" using column numbers makes the ARG instruction extremely powerful. Here is another example that shows how the numbers in the template can be used:

```
ARG 1 abd 1 def 1 ghi 1 jkl
```

This takes the input argument string and assigns it to each variable, thus eliminating the need for several assignment statements in the program. Additional column numbers can be used also; if the input argument string contained "The boy threw the ball to the dog" and the following ARG statement was used:

```
ARG 1 full 1 subject 8 1 subject_article 4
```

it would place the entire sentence into the variable *full*, the string "THE BOY" into the variable *subject*, and the string "THE" into the variable *subject_article*.

Quite often, the mini-template is used to avoid having to code additional statements, be they additional (PARSE) ARG instructions or some of the built-in functions, such as SUBSTR() or WORD(). The point to keep in mind about a technique such as this is that someone who is new to REXX may not fully digest the power of the statement. To help this situation (should it come up in the future), use comments to explain how the statement is being used. Tricks are not "bad"; it's just easier for others if they are alerted to the fact that a trick is being used.

14.1.2.3 Numbers in the template—signed

Both signed and unsigned numbers can be used in a template. The use of the + or - sign in front of a number causes REXX to take the starting position of the variable or synchronization string that precedes the signed number, and move in the direction of the sign the number of character positions (+ means to the right, - means to the left). This give you an extremely powerful method of searching for values using the (PARSE) ARG instruction.

One of the more important points to make at this time is that using a signed number in a template following a synchronization string causes the string to remain and be parsed into variables. This is contrasted with using an unsigned number, which causes the string to be removed, and thus not parsed into any of the template variables.

14.1.2.4 Variables in parentheses in the template

From time to time, you may find yourself writing templates that use the same synchronization character string several times throughout your program. Or you may find that you need to use several rather long synchronization strings on your template. Instead of repeating the string several times or using the several long quoted strings in the template, you can use a variable to hold the string itself. Simply place the variable in the template, along with the other variables, but place it in parentheses.

But I thought any variable in the template is going to get filled in with some value, you might be thinking. That's correct, unless a given variable is enclosed within parentheses. The presence of the parentheses tells REXX to "look up the value of this variable that is contained in parentheses, and use the value as if it were placed in quotes in the template."

This technique comes in quite handy at times. For instance, if there are several strings that are going to be used to parse a given input argument string, the synchronization characters may be placed in variables, and those variables can then be used in the template, shortening the physical length of the template and thus increasing readability of that (PARSE) ARG instruction. Of course, there would be a need for some additional assignment statements, but that is the trade off one has to make in an attempt to make the template more understandable. This view is more of a long-range view, which includes empathy for those who might inherit this particular program at some point in the future.

A second way of looking at using the variable inside the template is the case where an input argument string might use different delimiters each time it is run. For example, let's assume a program is to handle two different input argument strings, one representing date input in the form of xx/xx/xx, and one representing clock time in the form of xx:xx:xx. It is possible to have two separate ARG instructions, but consider this:

```
(PARSE) ARG 3 delim 4 1 first (delim) second (delim) third
```

The first part of the template assumes the argument string to be in the first position. This is not always the case. What is needed, then, is a more flexible template. One that would look at the string as blank-delimited words would be very handy, but once you start using signed numbers in the template, things change to character position. In this case, you would need an additional statement to get rid of the leading blanks. After that point, you can pick up the delimiter character as the third character in the string, and use that variable in parentheses for the remainder of the string.

The use of variables inside parentheses is just one way of handling potentially sticky situations when parsing input argument strings.

14.1.2.5 Variables in parentheses with a sign in front

This is a rather obscure method of parsing that is supported in REXX in OS/2.   It allows a special character to be placed immediately in front of the parentheses (the left one of the pair) that enclose a variable in a template. The three characters are used this way:

+ **(var)**   The variable **var** contains a numeric value that is to be used as a relative character position as if +3 (if **var** had been assigned the value 3) had been specified in the template.

```
parse var abc x +3 y
```

and

```
parse var abc x +(var) y
```

are equivalent.

-**(var)**   The variable **var** contains a numeric value that is to be used as a relative character position as if -3 (if **var** had been assigned the value 3) had been specified in the template.

```
parse var abc x -3 y
```

and

```
parse var abc x -(var) y
```

are equivalent.

= **(var)**   The variable **var** contains a numeric value that is to be used as an absolute character position as if 3 (if **var** had been assigned the value 3) had been specified in the template.

```
parse var abc x 3   y
```

and

```
parse var abc x =(var) y
```

are equivalent.

14.1.2.6 The period (.) in the template

Instead of using a number of variable names in the template (not enclosed by parentheses) to hold values that you do not really want for your program during a given run, it is possible to use a period in place of a variable at any point in a template. The period is looked upon as "accept whatever value(s) would have gone in here if there were a real variable at this spot in the template." Now, we all know that the period is not a valid variable name. It can be used *in* a variable name, of course, but is not valid as a variable name (in and of itself). However, the (PARSE) ARG instruction treats it as if it were a variable, in order to split up the input argument string the way the template was designed.

There can be any number of periods in a template. However, there must be at least one blank on either side of the period. If there is not, the period may actually create a stem of a compound variable; stems are allowed in the template. Therefore, you must be careful when using periods in the template.

14.1.3 While the Program Is Running

Once you have decided that the input arguments are to be supplied separate from the invocation of the program, there are a few choices that are available to you. They all center around the idea of a "prompt and response" approach. The program will have to prompt the user for some input, and when the user presses Enter, that response needs to be picked up in order for the program to be able to process those arguments.

Note: TSO/E REXX users: This use of *prompt* is not referring to *prompt mode* for interactive TSO/E commands. Here, it is being used to mean "instructing the user to enter" information.

The prompting and capturing of the response is typically done using the SAY instruction to display the prompt (the request for information) and the (PARSE) PULL instruction (for CMS and TSO/E users, the PARSE EXTERNAL instruction is also available; for OS/2 users, the LINEIN() function is used).

14.1.3.1 Synchronization strings

When looking at the input argument string (the response from the user), there may be times that you need to have the user supply information in the form *keyword = value* in order to "help keep things straight."   In this case, the template can look like this: (shown with the PULL instruction) *PULL ARG kwd ' = ' kwdval*. This causes the template to "line up" or "synchronize" itself at the ' = ', thus giving two *mini-templates*.   The response can be looked at as being split into two separate groups, and the values that go into the variables would be the input argument string (without the ' = '). In the basic template (no numbers used in the template), the synchronization string is not used as values for the template variables.   Its purpose here is to split up the template into mini-templates. This rule applies unless there is a signed number following the synchronization string. See Sec. 14.1.3.2, "Numbers in the template—unsigned," for an explanation.

There can be any number of mini-templates; keep in mind that the practical limit is controlled by the length of the input argument string that can be supplied by the user.

The synchronization string can be more than one character in length.   It does not make sense to have the string be of greater length than the input argument string itself, however.

14.1.3.2 Numbers in the template—unsigned

In addition to having a synchronization string in a template for the (PARSE) PULL instruction, numbers are allowed. They direct REXX by identifying where the variables' fields start in the input argument string. For example,

```
ARG 1 abc 10 def 15 ghi
```

will cause REXX to put the characters in columns $1-9$ (inclusive) in the variable abc, the characters from columns $10-14$ (inclusive) in the variable def, and the rest of the values into the last variable on the template (columns 15 to the end).   A slightly different way of looking at this template is to read it as

> The field for abc starts in column 1; the field for def starts in column 10; the field for ghi starts in column 15.

There is an implied '1' at the beginning of the template when column numbers are used.

There can be more than one variable between the column position numbers. In this case, the template is effectively split into mini-templates, and the normal rules of parsing apply (split by blanks, start from the left, the last variable in that *mini*-template receives all the rest of the values, etc.). In addition, synchronization strings can be used in the template along with column position numbers. Thus, you can have several mini-templates, based on how you want to split the data.

A not-so-obvious use of numbers in a template is the ability to take a "second pass" over the data. For example,

```
PULL fn ft fm 1 first_char 2
```

will take the data items and parse them into fn, ft, and fm, *then* go back to column a and place the character in column 1 into the variable **first_char**. If the column position numbers were not used, then the variable(s) that hold(s) the response would have to be PARSEd; this is different from the ARG instruction, which can be issued several times in the same section of the program (from a point of view of internal subroutines and functions). You can get the response (in a prompt and response mode) from the user only once; each time you go after the response, the user has to re-enter it. The ability to "go back" using column numbers makes the PULL instruction extremely powerful. Here is another example that shows how the numbers in the template can be used:

```
PULL 1 abc 1 def 1 ghi 1 jkl
```

This takes the response and assigns it to each variable, thus eliminating the need for several assignment statements in the program. Additional column numbers can be used also; if the response contained "The boy threw the ball to the dog" and the following PULL statement was used:

```
PULL full 1 subject 8 1 subject_article 4
```

REXX would place the entire sentence into the variable **full**, the string "THE BOY" into the variable **subject**, and the string "THE" into the variable **subject_article**.

Quite often, the mini-template is used to avoid having to code additional statements, be they additional (PARSE) PULL instructions or some of the built-in functions, such as SUBSTR() or WORD(). The point to keep in mind about a technique such as this is that someone who is new to REXX may not fully digest the power of the statement. To help this situation (should it come up in the future), use comments to explain how the statement is being used. Tricks are not "bad"; it's just easier for others if they are alerted to the fact that a trick is being used.

14.1.3.3 Numbers in the template—signed

Both signed and unsigned numbers can be used in a template. The use of the + or - sign in front of a number causes REXX to take the starting position of the variable or synchronization string that precedes the signed number, and move in the direction of the sign the number of character positions (+ means to the right, - means to the left). This gives you an extremely powerful method of searching for values using the (PARSE) PULL instruction.

One of the more important points to make at this time is that using a signed number in a template following a synchronization string causes the string to remain and be parsed into variables. This is contrasted with using an unsigned number, which causes the string to be removed, and thus not parsed into any of the template variables.

14.1.3.4 Variables in parentheses in the template

From time to time, you may find yourself writing templates that use the same synchronization character string several times throughout your program. Or you may find that you need to use several rather long synchronization strings on your template. Instead of repeating the string several times or using the several long quoted strings in the template, you can use a variable to hold the string itself. Simply place the variable in the template, along with the other variables, but place it in parentheses.

But I thought any variable in the template is going to get filled in with some value, you might be thinking. That's correct, unless a given variable is enclosed within parentheses. The presence of the parentheses tells REXX to "look up the value of this variable that is contained in parentheses, and use the value as if it were placed in quotes in the template."

This technique comes in quite handy at times. For instance, if there are several strings that are going to be used to parse a given response, the synchronization characters may be placed in variables, and those variables can then be used in the template, shortening the physical length of the template, and thus increasing readability of that (PARSE) ARG instruction. Of course, there would be a need for some additional assignment statements, but that is the trade-off one has to make in an attempt to make the template more understandable. This view is more of a long-range view, which includes empathy for those who might inherit this particular program at some point in the future.

A second way of looking at using the variable inside the template is the case where a response might use different delimiters each time it is run. For example, let's assume a program is to handle two different responses, one representing date input in the form of xx/xx/xx, and one representing clock time in the form of xx:xx:xx. It is possible to have two separate PULL instructions, each with the '/' or the ':' as the synchronization string; but consider this:

```
(PARSE) PULL 3 delim 4 1 first (delim) second (delim) third
```

The first part of the template assumes the response to be in the first position. This is not always the case. What is needed, then, is a more flexible template. One that would look at the string as blank-delimited words would be very handy, but once you start using signed numbers in the template, things change to character position. In this case, you would need an additional statement to get rid of the leading blanks. After that point, you can pick up the delimiter character as the third character in the string, and use that variable in parentheses for the remainder of the string.

The use of variables inside the parentheses is just one way of handling potentially sticky situations when parsing responses.

14.1.3.5 Variables in parentheses with a +, -, or = in front of them

This is a rather obscure method of parsing that is supported in REXX in OS/2. It allows a special character to be placed immediately in front of the parenthesis (the left one of the pair) that encloses a variable in a template. The three characters are used this way:

+(var)   The variable **var** contains a numeric value that is to be used as a relative character position as if +3 (if **var** had been assigned the value 3) had been specified in the template.

```
parse var abc x +3 y
```

and

```
parse var abc x +(var) y
```

are equivalent.   ~

-(var)   The variable **var** contains a numeric value that is to be used as a relative character position as if -3 (if **var** had been assigned the value 3) had been specified in the template.

```
parse var abc x -3 y
```

and

```
parse var abc x -(var) y
```

are equivalent.

=(var)   The variable **var** contains a numeric value that is to be used as an absolute character position as if 3 (if **var** had been assigned the value 3) had been specified in the template.

```
parse var abc x 3  y
```

and

```
parse var abc x =(var) y
```

are equivalent.

14.1.3.6 The period (.) in the template

Instead of using a number of variable names in the template (not enclosed by parentheses) to hold values that you do not really want for your program during a given run, it is possible to use a period in place of a variable at any point in a template. The period is looked upon as "accept whatever value(s) would have gone in here if there were a real variable at this spot in the template." Now, we all know that the period is not a valid variable name. It can be used *in* a variable name, of course, but it is not valid as a variable name (in and of itself). However, the (PARSE) PULL instruction treats it as if it were a variable, in order to split up the input argument string the way the template was designed.

There can be any number of periods in a template. However, there must be at least one blank on either side of the period. If there is not, the period may actually create a stem of a compound variable; stems are allowed in the template. Therefore, you must be careful when using periods in the template.

14.2 Handling Default Values

When handling input arguments, there are times when you want the variable(s) to take on a value that will be used if the user does not supply a specific value. Most often, this is referred to as "taking a default value." There are many ways in which this can be accomplished. Based on the template used on the ARG instruction, if the user does not provide certain values, the variables will be set to the null string. An example of code that handles this situation and fills the variable in with the default value follows:

```
if file_extension = '' then file_extension= '.EXE'
```

This straightforward method is commonly found in many programs. Here's a slightly different way. It takes advantage of the fact that a variable might have been assigned the null string. Here's a slightly different example:

```
file_extension=word(file_extension  '.EXE',1)
```

The contents of the variable **file_extension** are *blank concatenated* to the string .EXE, yielding a two-word string (yes, there could be more than two if the variable had been assigned more than one value, but here we are concerned more with the case where the null string has been assigned). Remember, REXX will evaluate whatever is between the parentheses before passing any values from the resulting string to the function. The WORD() function will take the first word in that string. If there is a value inside the variable **file_extension**, that value will be the first word in the resulting string, and it will be placed back on top of itself. If the variable had been assigned the null string, then you would be concatenating a null string to one word (the string .EXE), and you would be left with a resulting string that consists only of the default value (it is similar to adding nothing to something; you get the same something that you started with).

In addition to simply specifying the first word of the string, you can make use of the WORD() function to selectively choose one word from a string of words by using a little arithmetic and Boolean logic. For example, suppose you want to take one of two values based on another value being within a certain range of numbers.

```
chosen=word('RTN1 RTN2',input_value> 12)
```

Now, this example would go after word 1 if the input value was greater than 12, but there would be a slight problem if the input value was less than or equal to 12. That would return a 0, and the word() function cannot handle a word position designation of 0. The way to avoid this problem is to make use of a "base and displacement" technique. Take the logical expression as it stands, and let that determine the displacement. To that quantity, add the base. Here's how we can correct the previous example:

```
chosen=word('RTN1 RTN2',(input_value> 12)+1)
```

This will now ensure that the WORD() function is fed either a 1 or a 0, right? Wrong. There is nothing shown here to ensure that the value inside the input variable is an integer. There are several ways to accomplish this. The DATATYPE() function comes to mind, but there is also a slight modification to the statement so that it takes the value inside the input variable and makes it into an integer:

```
chosen=word('RTN1 RTN2',((input_value> 12)+)%1)
```

Of course, variables can be used to build the string that is passed as the first argument to the WORD() function.

Chapter 15.
Reading/Writing Files

When reading from files or writing to files, there are several items to keep in mind:

- How to specify the file (its name, etc.)
- How to know when to stop reading/writing
- How to read and write to the same file
- Where to place the lines for/from the file

These will be looked at for the CMS, TSO/E, and OS/2 environments.

15.1 CMS

In the CMS environment, a file is looked at as a collection of records that can be read as one entire group, read individually (in sequential manner), read directly ("read record number 4"), or read as a group of records ("read 20 records, starting at record number 10"). The same view is used for writing a file also. Simply re-read this paragraph, and replace the word *read* with *write*.

In the CMS environment, REXX has no "native" input/output capability, so a host command is needed. As with any host command, the variable RC is used to determine whether things worked correctly or not.

15.1.1 What Do I Use to Read/Write Files?

Use the EXECIO command. It is a CMS command.

15.1.2 How to Specify the File (Its Name, Etc.)

In CMS, a file is referred to by its label, which consists of three parts: the filename, the filetype, and the filemode. The filename and filetype are each a string of 1 to 8 characters. The characters for the filename and filetype can be any of the following:

- Numerals $0-9$
- @, #, -, :, or _
- Upper case $A-Z$
- Lower case $A-Z$

Note: CMS supports mixed and lower case fileids. EXECIO supports them also. However, there may be other commands you want to use against that file that might not support mixed or lower case fileids.

The filemode consists of one letter (upper case $A-Z$), followed by a numeral $(0-6)$. The letter represents the minidisk (or Shared File System Directory) upon which the file resides. The numeral defines what *type* of file it is. In general terms, a filemode number of 1, 2, 4, or 5 can be thought of as "regular." The other filemode numbers are as follows:

0   Private. If another userid has access to the files on this minidisk or directory, files with mode 0 will be hidden from that user.

3   Temporary. Once a file that has a filemode number of 3 has been created, you are allowed to access it once (to edit, browse, read, etc.). Once you have accessed it, the file is automatically erased. If you are editing the file with XEDIT, you can issue the XEDIT FILE command, and the file will not be erased once you return from XEDIT.

6   Update in place. For most cases, this can be thought of as "regular," but close attention needs to be paid when more than one user has write access to that file.

15.1.3 How to Know When to Stop Reading/Writing

The EXECIO command can be used in one of two ways:

- Reading the whole file at once
- Reading a part of a file each time (can be a single record or a group of records)

Knowing when to stop is different for each way. In either case, the variable **rc** is used to determine whether to stop or not. When you are reading the whole file at once, EXECIO will return with a return code of 0, which gets placed in the variable **rc**. You can think of it in this way: you told EXECIO to read the entire file, and it did.

When you are reading a part of a file, be it one record or more than one, EXECIO will return a return code of 2 when you have tried to read past the end of the file. This is your signal to stop reading the file (unless, of course, your program is designed to go back and re-read parts of the file).

15.1.4 How to Read and Write to the Same File

In CMS, you do not have to do anything at all in order to be able to read from and write to the same file. However, there are some considerations dealing with the point in the file at which you will be reading or writing.

If you want to *write* to a file, but you do not specify the line number, the record that you write will be placed at the next available record position in the file. If you write to the file before reading it, the next available record will be the record following the last record on the file (in other words, records you write to the file will be appended to the file). This will happen whether or not you have read the file previously.

If you want to *write* to a file, and you do specify the line number, that particular record gets updated with the new data you specify. If you are dealing with a file that has variable-length records, you must be careful; if you update a particular record with one that is of unequal length, you will lose the remainder of the file. The way the "pointer to the next record in the file" is kept, replacing the record with one that is of unequal length (to the original) will cause the pointer to be ignored (if the length is less than the original) or overwritten (if the length is greater than original), thus losing contact with the rest of the file. You must update a record in a variable-length record file with a record that is of equal length.

If you want to *write* to a file, and you specify a line number that is beyond the end of the file, EXECIO will add as many blank lines as needed to "fill in the gap," and then write your record.

If you want to *read* a file, and you read the entire file, you must close the file before you are able to read the entire file again. This can be done by using the FINIS option of EXECIO, or it can be done by using the CMS FINIS command. This is because the file pointer has been placed past the end of the file. You will still get a return code of 0, but no records from the file will be read.

If you want to *read* a file, and you specify the line number at which to begin reading, you don't have to close the file before going after the file again. Specifying the line number is a safeguard against the file pointer being placed at a point past the end of the file.

15.1.5   Where to Place the Lines for/from the File

There are two places that data for/from records can be placed: the Program Stack or variables (you have your choice of simple or compound variables). The Program Stack is used by default. You have to use the VAR or STEM option to read into simple and compound variables, respectively.

If you use the Program Stack, you are limited to reading the *first* 255 columns from each record read. As long as your file has a width that is less than or equal to 255 characters, you've got no problem. If the file is wider than 255 characters, there is no way to read the 256th (and beyond) character from any record in the file; the MARGINS and ZONE options will not help you out with this limitation. In this case, you should consider the VAR or STEM option.

The VAR option should be used when you have one record to read or write. EXECIO allows only a 1 to be specified as the number of records to process when using the VAR option. This can be used in some sort of loop structure, to process the file sequentially.

The STEM option should be used to read in a portion of the file, or the whole file at once. Whatever you specify as the stem will have a number appended to the name. For example,

```
EXECIO * DISKR TEST FILE A (STEM X.'
```

will create the variables **x.1, x.2, x.3, etc.**, with each compound variable containing a record from the file. The variable **x.0** will contain the number of records that were read from the file. If you specify a simple variable,

```
EXECIO * DISKR TEST FILE A (STEM X'
```

The variables **x1, x2, x3, etc.** will be created.   The variable **x0** will contain the number of records read.   Note the lack of the period (which would have made this example one containing compound and not simple variables). Any string that is valid for making into a variable name can be specified; therefore

```
EXECIO * DISKR TEST FILE A (STEM X.1.'
```

will create the variables **x.1.1, x.1.2, x.1.3, etc.**   The variable **x.1.0** will contain the number of records read. Using this latter technique, one could (conceivably) execute some EXECIO commands against the same file with different settings for the STEM option and the MARGINS options. For example,

```
'EXECIO * DISKR TEST FILE A 1 (STEM X.1. MARGINS 10 20'
'EXECIO * DISKR TEST FILE A 1 (STEM X.2. MARGINS 30 50'
```

will "split" the file records into two groups, the first being the set of data found in columns $10-20$ (inclusive), and the second being the set of data found in columns $30-50$ (inclusive). The table **x.** is now created, with two columns and **x.1.0** rows (or **x.2.0** rows). This technique allows the creation of a two-dimensional table from the EXECIO command.

15.2 TSO/E

In the TSO/E environment, a file is looked at as a collection of records that can be read as one entire group, read individually (in sequential manner), read directly ("read record number 4"), or read as a group of records ("read 20 records, starting at record number

10″).   The same view is used for writing a file also.   Simply re-read this paragraph, and replace the word *read* with *write*.

In the TSO/E environment, REXX has no "native" input/output capability, so a host command is needed.   As with any host command, the variable RC is used to determine whether things worked correctly or not.

15.2.1   What Do I Use to Read/Write Files?

Use the EXECIO command.   It is a TSO/E command.   It is similar to the CMS EXECIO command in its general structure.   In TSO/E, you write/read a *data set*.   It gives you the choice of reading/writing file records to/from either the stack or compound variables.

15.2.2   How to Specify the File (Its Name, Etc.)

In TSO/E, the data set that you want to read/write may be a member of a partitioned data set (PDS), or it may be a sequential data set.   The data set must be ALLOCATEd to a file (a *ddname*). The file to which the data set has been allocated is specified on the EXECIO statement.

The name of the PDS consists of four parts: Project.Group.Type(Member).   Each part of the name can be a maximum of eight characters.   For many users, the PROJECT name will coincide with the userid (this is not always the case, however).   If the parentheses are not used, but a period is used to separate the MEMBER from the TYPE, the file is considered to be a sequential data set, and thus has no "members."

The characters that can be used in the name of a PDS are alphabetic characters, numbers, the dollar sign ($), the pound sign (#), and the "at" sign (@).   The first character in each part can be any of these, except for numbers.

15.2.3   How to Know When to Stop Reading/Writing

The EXECIO command will return a return code of 2 if processing the file sequentially (record by record) or as a group (but not by using * for the number or records to process).   If the * is specified, the return code will be 0, saying "ok, I read all the rest of the records from the file."

When writing records to a file from compound variables, the EXECIO command will stop writing once it encounters the null string or an uninitialized variable (one that looks like it was DROPped—has its name as its value). This behavior is slightly different from that of the EXECIO available with CMS. With either, you can specify the number of lines to read/write by specifying the number directly (hard-coded) or through a variable.

15.2.4 How to Read and Write to the Same File

Using the EXECIO command, a file can be updated (read from and written to). Use the DISKRU form of EXECIO. In this mode (you can think of it as update mode), you can update only the last record read. You have the capability of updating a specific record in a data set, but you have to issue the EXECIO DISKRU against that record first. Therefore, it takes two EXECIO commands to update a record in a file (data set). For example,

```
'EXECIO 1 DISKRU 'infile which_line' (STEM X.'
x.1=overlay(new_string, old_string, where, length)
'EXECIO 1 DISKW ' infile which_line' (FINIS STEM X.'
```

will update the which_lineth record of infile. Following the writing of the new version of the record, the file is closed. The closing of the file after each read or write is asking quite a bit of the system, and should be avoided; just don't forget to close the file once you're done.

The length of the new version of the record should match the length of the old version of the record. If the length of the new version is too short, it will be padded with blanks. If it is too long, it will be truncated. If the record is truncated, EXECIO will return a return code of 1. This may or may not be an "error" to your program—that's for you to decide. Updating a record in a file is doing just that, updating the record—not just one of the fields in a record.

15.2.5 Where to Place the Lines for/from the File

The records from the files are read into the stack, or into variables (simple or compound). The records can be read in as a group or individually. The entire record is read, as opposed to the width of the stack being the delimiting factor. When reading the file, you have the option of specifying the line number at which to start reading. When writing the file, this is not available; either you append records to the end of the file, or you update an individual record that you just read with DISKRU.

15.3 OS/2

In the OS/2 environment, a file is looked at as a "stream" of characters that can be read record by record or read directly ("read record number 15"). The reading of the stream is done by the LINEIN() function. The same view is used for writing a file also. Simply re-read this paragraph, and replace the word *read* with *write* and LINEIN() with LINEOUT().

15.3.1 What Do I Use to Read/Write Files?

In the OS/2 environment, REXX has the LINEIN() and LINEOUT() functions for reading a file as a stream of records. The CHARIN() and CHAROUT() functions are available for reading a file as a stream of characters. Reading the file as a stream of records "honors" the end-of-record separator that exists between records. Reading the file as a stream of characters does not "honor" the end-of-record separator; instead, it is one of the characters that can be brought in from the file, and depending on the purpose of your program, may or may not be considered an invalid value.

The LINEIN() and LINEOUT() functions allow you to specify a starting point and the number of records to read/write, along with the name of the file. The starting point and number of records are optional pieces of information you can feed to the function. If you do not specify them, they default to "one record at a time, in sequential fashion."

15.3.2 How to Specify the File (Its Name, Etc.)

To ensure that your file picks the correct file to process (read or write), make sure you match the case of the filename, and specify it in its fully qualified form; this way, there is no question as to which file is being sought. It will be easier to set the name of the file in a variable, and use that variable as an "alias" for that file throughout the program.

OS/2 has two file systems: the File Allocation Table (FAT) file system, and the High-Performance File System (HPFS). There are reserved words which cannot be used in the filename, and there are special characters that cannot be used in the filename. The reserved words are the same for both file systems:

        CLOCK$
        COM1
        COM2
        COM3
        CON
        KBD$
        LPT1
        LPT2
        LPT3
        MOUSE$
        NUL
        POINTER$
        PRN
        SCREEN$

The reserved special characters are:

HPFS   " / \ :] < > , ?
FAT   the above, plus ffl " ; + = *

The FAT file system allows for an (up to) eight-character filename with an optional extension that has (up to) three characters. The extension is separated from the filename by a period. A maximum of one period is allowed in the filename of a FAT file system file.

The HPFS file system allows a name that can contain several periods, with a maximum overall length (periods included) of 254 characters.

15.3.3 How to Know When to Stop Reading/Writing

In OS/2, the reading/writing of files is done through the use of functions, as opposed to host commands. Thus, the concept of "check the value of RC" does not apply. The view that should be taken is "are there any more records left to process?" This is accomplished with the LINES() function. Use it to determine when to stop processing an input file. For example,

```
file='STARTUP.CMD'
do forever
   parse value linein(file) with a b c d e
   if lines(file)=0 then leave

   ⋮

   /* process the file record */
end
```

makes use of the LINES() function to see whether there are any more records left in the stream. The same applies to the CHARIN() approach. Here, the CHARS() function will tell you if there are any more characters left in the stream to process.

This is a bit of a change for those who have written REXX programs in the CMS and/or TSO/E environments, but a little change now and then can be interesting.

15.3.4 How to Read and Write to the Same File

The safest way to read and write to the same file is to read the file into compound variables, update whatever is to be updated, and write the file out. The LINEIN() and LINEOUT() functions do not take the approach of "read in a file record, and then let me update that record using the LINEOUT() function."

If you are writing records to the end of a file, the LINEOUT() function is just what you need. Simply don't specify a value for the line at which to start, and it will begin adding records to the end of the file.

If you are writing records to update an entire file (starting from the first record), specify a 1 for the line at which to start; thereafter, the LINEOUT() functions that don't have a line number specified will continue writing at the record following the previously written one.

15.3.5 Where to Place the Lines for/from the File

With the main tool for reading files being the LINEIN() and LINEOUT() functions, the values will be most easily directed to/from variables. This fits in with the REXX view of input records as a "stream" of records, and the invocation of the

LINEIN() function returning the next piece of the stream. Given this model, you read one line at a time with LINEIN(), and you write one line at a time with the LINEOUT() function. If you want to read a block of lines or write a block of lines, you will need to use a loop structure. Using compound variables will be most handy here. For example, to take and read in a file called TECHNOID.SIS into compound variables with the stem FAMILY., the following code will work nicely:

```
file='TECHNOID.SIS'
do i=1 until LINES(file)=0
   family.i=LINEIN(file)
end
family.0=i-1
```

Figure 62. Reading a block of lines using LINEIN().

When this loop completes, the variable i will have a value that is one more than the number of records read. This is because when there is a compound condition being tested on the loop, each part of that condition is tested, from left to right. In other words, the i = 1 part of the loop is tested first. Since the "loop control variable" type of loop is treated as increment the counter, and then test to see if the final value has been exceeded, i gets incremented, and, since there is no final value specified, is treated as a true condition. This causes REXX to look at the next part of the condition, namely the until LINES(file) = 0 part of the condition. Once that condition turns out to be true, the loop terminates; however, the loop control variable has already been incremented. Thus, the value of "one more than the number of times through the loop."

15.4 Can I Use LINEIN() and LINEOUT in CMS or TSO?

From the standpoint of portability, it would be nice if the LINEIN() and LINEOUT() functions were available in REXX on CMS and TSO. In their absence, the following routines provide the basic framework around which LINEIN() and LINEOUT can exist in a REXX environment that does not have them. While they don't necessary follow *all* the behaviors of the functions in the OS/2 environment, they lay the groundwork for explaining their basic behaviors.

```
LINEIN: procedure
arg name, line, count
if arg() <> 0
  then
    do
      'EXECIO 1 DISKR' name' (STEM INLINE.'
      if line = '' | line = 1 | count = 0
        then nop
        else inline.1=''
    end
  else pull inline.1
return inline.1
LINEOUT: procedure
arg name, string.1, line
if string = ''
  then 'EXECIO 0 DISKW' name' (FINIS'
  else 'EXECIO 1 DISKW' name' (STEM STRING.'
if rc <> 0
  then error = 1
  else error=0
return error
```

Figure 63. Invoke program, and supply all inputs at the start.

Chapter 16.
Using Select in Place of IF

16.1 The IF Statement

Basically, an IF instruction is used to make a single decision. You have the option of executing the code on the THEN branch or the code on the ELSE branch. If the ELSE is not specified, then your decision is to perform the code on the THEN branch or not to execute it. Either way, the decision is a single one.

IF statements can be nested on either branch of the IF. This allows the program writer a great deal of flexibility in structuring the program logic. When nesting IF statements, be careful to ensure that there is a sufficient number of ELSE statements to balance the program segment in a way that not only matches the intended logic, but also lends itself to being easily modified or enhanced in the future. It is possible to end up with a nested IF structure that is very difficult to read and/or difficult to maintain. For example,

```
if A = '1'
  then call xyz
  else
   if A = '2'
     then if rc = '1'
             then say 'ERROR1'
             else if rc ='28'
                    then say 'ERROR28'
                    else nop
        else if A = '3'
                then call def
                else call abc
```

could easily become unwieldy if checks were needed for many
return codes when the variable **a** had a value of 2.

16.2   The SELECT Statement

The SELECT instruction, in contrast, allows for many decisions to
be made in a way that follows the physical flow of the statement
as it is written.   The SELECT statement uses a WHEN branch
(which can be thought of as the IF-THEN part of the IF
statement).   When the expression is true, the action following that
WHEN is executed.   This action can be a single REXX
instruction, a subroutine call, a host command, or a DO...END (a
DO group) that includes any of these.   The WHENs are taken in
physical sequence; the first one coded is the first one checked.   If
the expression is not true, the next WHEN is checked.   This is
similar to having several IFs, one right after the other, but
without any ELSEs.   It is a drop-through structure; if a particular
IF statement is false, and there is no ELSE to execute, simply
continue with the program—drop through to the next statement.

   This is similar, but not the same.   In the SELECT instruction,
once a WHEN expression is true, the SELECT is terminated.
Control of the program goes to the line following the END that
corresponds to the SELECT.   In other words, you check only until
you find a true expression.   With IF statements, once one IF
executes, the next one is executed.   Unless there is an EXIT or
RETURN (or an equally terminating kind of instruction) found in
the THEN branch of an IF statement, each IF statement in that
section of the program would have to be executed, which will most
likely cause unnecessary cycles for REXX.   The SELECT makes

REXX ask questions only until it gets an expression that yields a 1 (representing TRUE).

There is one point about the SELECT instruction that should not be forgotten. If it is at all possible to "fall through" all of the WHEN expressions, you are required to have an OTHERWISE clause following the last WHEN in the SELECT. If you have "covered all bases" in the coding of the WHENs, then the OTHERWISE is not needed, because you can be assured that one of the WHENs will be executed during each trip through the SELECT.   Ensuring that you have "covered all bases" with the WHENs is sometimes neither possible nor desirable. The WHENs can check *any* expression that evaluates to a 1 or a 0 (which is something that sets it apart from CASE statements found in some other languages; they limit the checking to various values for one variable). In such cases, an OTHERWISE clause would be needed. It does not have to do anything in particular; if that's what you want, code an OTHERWISE NOP at the end of the SELECT.

Suggestion: At the very least, always code an OTHERWISE, even if it is not needed.   This will facilitate any future modifications (and act as a safeguard in case someone makes a change such that now "not all the bases are covered."

The SELECT instruction lends itself to a more vertical programming style that helps reduce the indentation levels in the program.   This vertical style makes it much easier to modify the conditions being tested. Using the previous example of nested IFs, we can see that by using the SELECT statement, the code reads more smoothly:

```
select
  when A = '1' then call xyz
  when A = '2' then
      select
        when rc = '1' then say 'ERROR1'
        when rc ='28' then say 'ERROR28'
        otherwise nop
      end
  when A = '3' then call def
  otherwise
      call abc
end
```

Use the IF statement if you are making a decision, and will choose between only two actions. If more than two actions are to be considered, or if more than one expression is to be tested, the SELECT will be a more effective way of coding those tests.

Chapter 17.
Setting Up Tables from a Data File

There may be times when you are dealing with files that contain data records that you need in your program (in the form of a table). In some cases, the data may be columnar (each field starts in the same character position on each record); if so, you can structure any templates using numeric character positions. If not, then you may have to use pattern matching strings, or simply rely on blank-delimited strings to parse the field values. You will need to perform the file I/O to accomplish this (see Chapter 15, "Reading/Writing Files" for the basics of file I/O for your environment). However, there are some considerations that must be made to set up your tables.

17.1 Setting Up Tables Using the EXECIO Command

17.1.1 Tables by EXECIO in CMS

If you are dealing with columnar data, then the MARGINS option of EXECIO will come in handy. Keeping in mind that the STEM option will produce only a single-dimension table, one can use the MARGINS option during an execution of EXECIO to select one or more fields from a file record. The MARGINS option allows you to specify a range of columns. For example,

```
'EXECIO * DISKR 'infile' 1 (FINIS STEM INPUT. MARGINS 10 20'
```

will read each record in the file, but will only place the characters in columns 10 to 20 (inclusive) into the table INPUT.

Using a slightly different stem, such as **input.1**, you can start to build a table that has more than one dimension. Consider the next three statements:

```
'EXECIO * DISKR 'infile' 1 (STEM INPUT.1. MARGINS 10 20'
'EXECIO * DISKR 'infile' 1 (STEM INPUT.2. MARGINS 30 40'
'EXECIO * DISKR 'infile' 1 (FINIS STEM INPUT.3. MARGINS 50 60'
```

These three statements build the table **INPUT.** as a table with three columns and **INPUT.1.0** rows. The data need to be columnar in order for this technique to work.

If the data are not columnar, then you need to have a loop structure that will allow you to read the file and parse each record in the file into the table variables. You have the choice of reading the entire file into storage at once or reading it in record by record. If you have the storage to support the entire file, the following code can be used to build the table:

```
'EXECIO * DISKR 'infile' 1 (FINIS STEM INPUT.'
do i = 1 to input.0
  parse var input.i 10 table.1.i 21 . 30 table.2.i 41 . 50 table.3.i 61
end
table.0=input.0
drop input.0
```

This will build **table.** with the same values as in our previous example. The use of the STEM option places the records into the **input.** table. The value in **input.0** is stored in **table.0**, and represents the number of rows in the table. The **input.** table is DROPped since it is no longer needed.

If you wanted to use the Program Stack, the PARSE VAR INPUT.i would become PARSE PULL; the template would stay the same. Keep in mind that the use of the Program Stack will limit you to the first 255 characters in each file record. In addition,

the INPUT. table would not exist, so it would not need to be
DROPped. Here is how the code would look if you were to use
the stack:

```
before=queued()  /* in case the stack already had some line on it */
'EXECIO * DISKR 'infile' 1 (FINIS'
number_of_lines=queued()-before
do i = 1 to number_of_lines
   parse pull 10 table.1.i 21 . 30 table.2.i 41 . 50 table.3.i 61
end
table.0=number_of_lines
```

17.1.2 Tables by EXECIO in TSO/E

In the EXECIO command in TSO/E, you have the choice of
reading the file into compound variables or into the stack. The
following code illustrates building the table from compound
variables:

```
'EXECIO * DISKR 'infile' 1 (STEM INPUT. FINIS'
do i = 1 to input.0
   parse var input.i 10 table.1.i 21 . 30 table.2.i 41 . 50 table.3.i 61
end
table.0=input.0
drop input.0
```

The decision between the use of compound variables and the
stack is not necessarily as clear in TSO/E as it is in VM. In VM,
the limit of 255 characters maximum on each line of the stack
would prove restricting in the context of "wide" input files (those
that have more than 255 characters per record). The stack in
TSO/E provides for a maximum of 16,777,215 characters per line.
Here is the code that can be used to read the file into the stack,
then use those lines to build the table:

```
before=queued()  /* in case the stack already had some line on it */
'EXECIO * DISKR 'infile' 1 (FINIS'
number_of_lines=queued()-before
do i = 1 to number_of_lines
   parse pull 10 table.1.i 21 . 30 table.2.i 41 . 50 table.3.i 61
end
table.0=number_of_lines
```

17.2 Setting Up Tables Using the LINEIN() Function

In keeping with the idea of an input file as a stream of input data to the program, the LINEIN() function can be used to read in a file and build a table with the file records. Here, the use of the LINEIN() function as part of a PARSE VALUE statement is what we want. Consider this example:

```
file='ABC.FIL'   /* assumes the file is in the same (sub)directory */
do record=1
   parse value linein(file) with ,
            10 table.1.i 21 . 30 table.2.i 41 . 50 table.3.i 61
   if lines(file)=0 then leave
end
table.0=record-1
```

This code builds the table TABLE. with 3 columns and table.0 rows.

In the LINEIN() environment, there are some things that need to be taken into consideration. The first (and perhaps the most important) is that the name of the file is taken as is; it is case-sensitive. Make certain that the case of the file as it is used in your program matches the case of the file from the host's point of view. Otherwise, it will not find the file you are asking for.

Second, there is no checking for a return code. We are using a function here, not a host command. In the absence of a host command to read our files and communicate through the variable RC, we have another function, LINES(), which tells us if we still have any records left to read. It does not tell us how many records there are (left); it simply asks the question "are there any records left to read?" Upon receiving a 0 from this function, we know we have reached the end of the file.

The file is read in, record by record, and each record is parsed onto the template. In this example, the template was placed on the next line, so line continuation was necessary.

The LINEIN() function reads a file in one record at a time, whereas the EXECIO command allows the entire file to be read onto the stack or directly into compound variables. It is a matter of style as to which one is "better."   There are positive and negative points to be made for each method.

Chapter 18.
Displaying Sparsely Populated Tables

Consider this: I have several files on a disk (or library). I want to list them in such a way that I can see, for a given size (in this example the blocksize will be used—a VM environment), how many files exist. For example, I want to know how many files take up only one block, how many take up two blocks, etc. I want to see only the blocksizes for which there are files. On any given day for any given person, there will not be a file for every blocksize from 1 to 1000; the most likely case is the one where there are some files that are one block, some that may be 10 blocks, a few that are 200 blocks—the point here is that the number of blocks that your files take up will most likely be a range from 1 to some relatively large number (in the hundreds, for instance), but if you were to take a list and tally off the files, you would have some "blocksizes" that would get no votes. This is what is meant by a sparsely populated table. Try this example on for size:

I have the following output from a LISTFILE * NOTEBOOK A command:

FILENAME	FILETYPE	FM	FORMAT	LRECL	RECS	BLOCKS	DATE	TIME
ALL	NOTEBOOK	A0	V	83	1677	18	10/19/90	14:20:40
ALLENSK	NOTEBOOK	A0	V	83	16	1	10/18/90	13:34:19
BASIC	NOTEBOOK	A0	V	83	28	1	10/18/90	13:34:27
FAST	NOTEBOOK	A0	V	73	103	2	10/18/90	13:23:17
GRAPHICS	NOTEBOOK	A0	V	83	213	3	9/18/90	11:55:11
MAGAZINE	NOTEBOOK	A0	V	83	67	1	10/05/90	15:35:39
NEWLIST	NOTEBOOK	A0	V	79	87	2	10/18/90	8:17:25
TECHNOID	NOTEBOOK	A0	V	83	213	4	7/02/90	16:52:23

I want to have a list that tells me how many files take up one block of disk space, how many take up two blocks, etc. You can see from this example that there are only a few (the list has been shortened for the purposes of this book). Here is the output I would like:

Blocks Used	How Many Files
1	3
2	2
3	1
4	1
18	1

Notice that the numbers from 1 to 4 were displayed, but then the table jumped to 18. This meant that there were no NOTEBOOK files that took up 5 to 17 blocks of disk space. This kind of information can help one manage disk space on an individual basis (which is something we all are concerned about at one point or another).

Here is the code that generated this output:

```
/*--HOWMANY EXEC-------------------------------------------------/
/-  syntax - HOWMANY fn ft fm                                  -/
/---------------------------------------------------------------*/
arg fn ft fm
fn=word(fn '*',1)
ft=word(ft '*',1)
fm=word(fm 'A',1)
blocklist.=0
/* stack the response from LISTFILE */
'LISTFILE' fn ft fm' (DATE STACK'
max=0
do queued()
   pull fn ft . . . . blocks .
   max=max(blocks,max)
   blocklist.blocks=blocklist.blocks + 1
end
say "Blocks Used      How Many Files"
say "===========      =============="
do i = 1 to max
   if blocklist.i > 0 then say center(i,11)||'        '||,
                            center(blocklist.i,14)
end
```

The variable **blocks** contains, on each trip through the loop, the number of blocks a particular file uses. Two lines further down, that value is used to set a particular element of the BLOCKLIST. table to a value which represents the number of times that particular number has "shown up" in the list. The table was initialized to 0; only the table elements used are being incremented. Also, the "highest value so far" is being chosen, which will give us our upper bound of the range of values. If the table were to be displayed from 1 to the maximum value used, there would be several 0s displayed as the file count. The ability to directly reference table elements gives us the opportunity to produce a sparsely populated table in a REXX program.

This example can be taken one step further. It can also produce the name of each file, to give you a better idea of which files are taking up a larger portion of the disk; you can then look at those files and determine their future (pruning, deletion, etc.). Here's how the code looks now. Again, it is set up for a small example; it will have to undergo further development to handle output of several names for one "block level."

```
/*--HOWMANY EXEC---------------------------------------------/
/- syntax - HOWMANY fn ft fm                                -/
/-----------------------------------------------------------*/
arg fn ft fm
fn=word(fn '*',1)
ft=word(ft '*',1)
fm=word(fm 'A',1)
blocklist.=0
/* Stack the response from LISTFILE */
'LISTFILE' fn ft fm' (DATE STACK'
max=0
do queued()
   pull fn ft . . . . blocks .
   max=max(blocks,max)
   blocklist.blocks=blocklist.blocks + 1
   if blocklist.blocks.name=0
     then blocklist.blocks.name= fn
     else blocklist.blocks.name= blocklist.blocks.name fn
end
say "Blocks Used      How Many Files      Which Ones"
say "===========      ==============      =========="
do i = 1 to max
   if blocklist.i > 0
     then say center(i,11)||'        '||center(blocklist.i,14)||,
                            '        '||blocklist.i.name
end
```

Again, we are taking advantage of the ability to directly reference the compound variables; we can add the second dimension to this table without any fanfare. The column represents the names of the files that are represented by the file count for each level of blocksize used. Since the table was initialized to 0, and that means that any variables that started with **blocklist.** would be given an initial value of 0, we use that in our check to say "if there have been no names found (up to this point) for this blocksize level, then set this name as the first one found; otherwise, add it to the list for that blocksize level."

Here is the output the modified version produces:

Blocks Used	How Many Files	Which Ones
1	3	ALLENSK BASIC MAGAZINE
2	2	FAST NEWLIST
3	1	GRAPHICS
4	1	TECHNOID
18	1	ALL

Chapter 19.
Finding an Available
Address or Mode (CMS)

19.1 Finding an Available Address

When dealing with minidisks, there are times when you need to be able to determine an available minidisk address. This can be accomplished in CMS by using the CP QUERY DASD command and the DIAG() function.

When dealing with tape drives, there are times when you need to be able to determine an available tape drive address. This can be accomplished in CMS by using the CP QUERY TAPE command and the DIAG() function.

Now, you may be wondering why a CP command is used to determine an available address for a minidisk, a tape, or some other device. In the context of tape drives, the tape drive is known only by its device address (for example, your 181 tape drive). In the context of the minidisk, the answer is found in the realization/remembrance that a minidisk is known by two names—its device address and the mode at which it is accessed. CP knows about the address itself; CMS concerns itself with the mode at which it is addressed. To CMS, it's your A-disk; to CP, it's your 191. We are focusing on the 191 aspect of a minidisk (or other device).

The DIAG() function is used to allow the command to be issued, and the command output to be trapped, without the need of the Program Stack. The DIAG() function will return the command output as the function result (which would most likely be placed in a variable). For example,

```
x=diag(8,'QUERY DASD')
```

will execute the command and place the command output (the lines that normally would go to the screen) in the variable x as a stream of characters, with a '15'x as the line separator between each line of output. This can then be used to set up a list of addresses as follows:

```
do i=1
   parse var x . addr.i . '15'x x   /* isolate address, in sequence */
   if x='' then leave
end
addr.0=i
```

This list of addresses can now be used to determine an available address. A loop that starts at an arbitrary address will come in handy. For example,

```
do i = 001
   found=0
   do j = 1 to addr.0
      if i=addr.j
        then
          do
            found=1
            leave
          end
   end
   if found=1
     then iterate
     else leave
end
```

will stop at the first address that is not in the ADDR. list. Since the list is the list of currently used addresses, the one not in the list is an available one.

You might be thinking that this is a bit of a cumbersome way to arrive at an available address. Consider, then, this next example:

```
do i = 001
   x=diag(8,'CP QUERY 'i)
   if rc¬=0 then leave
end
```

This example makes use of the CP QUERY command for each address that is being tried, until the first one is found that does not currently exist on your virtual machine. The DIAG() function is used to prevent the command output from being displayed on the screen. This method is more straightforward, and does not have the overhead of creating the table of addresses currently in use.

19.2 Finding an Available Access Mode

If what you need is an available access mode, the rules change. There are 26 modes that are available to you in the CMS environment. Twenty-five of these are available to you, the user. CMS reserves the right to use mode S for the CMS system disk.

To find an available access mode, consider the following example:

```
modes='ABCDEFGHIJKLMNOPQRTUVWXYZ'  /* note the absence of S */
'QUERY DISK (STACK'
pull                               /* remove the header     */
do queued()
   pull . . used_mode .
   modes=translate(modes,' ',used_mode)
end
modes=space(modes,0)
next_available_mode_at_top_of_alphabet=substr(modes,1,1)
next_available_mode_at_end_of_alphabet=substr(modes,length(modes),1)
```

The QUERY DISK command tells us what modes are currently in use. For those using some Shared File System directories, don't worry; the third column of information is still the access mode. The lone PULL instruction outside the loop is to remove the header line, since that would have taken M out of the list if it were processed along with the others. The space(___,0) removes any blanks between unused letters, creating one string of available modes. This allows the SUBSTR() and LENGTH() functions to be used to get the mode nearest the top of the alphabet (and thus

nearest the top of the search order) or to get the mode nearest the
bottom of the alphabet (the end of the search order).   Of course,
the reverse() function could have been used as follows:

```
next_available_mode_at_end_of_alphabet=substr(reverse(modes),1,1)
```

The Translate() and space() functions could also be combined:

```
modes=space(translate(modes,' ',used_mode),0)
```

Combining the functions (or nesting them, if you prefer) is one
way to even more powerful statements in your REXX program; it
is important to ensure that they are documented well enough in
case someone "inherits" the program in the future.

Chapter 20.
Can I Capture Host
Command Responses?

One of the strong points of REXX lies in its ability to issue host commands (if you prefer to think of it as having host commands issued, that's fine). Many host commands are designed to be displayed on the screen. This can be done even though the command is issued from within a REXX program. Each host command will place a return code value in the special REXX variable RC. However, there may be times, depending on the command issued, when the value inside RC may not be enough information for the program to complete its processing.

There may be a need to have the program "see" what is placed on the screen by a given command. This "seeing" may also be thought of as redirecting the command output to some place other than the screen. This is sometimes referred to as *capturing host command responses.*

The methods used to capture host command responses are different for each environment. Let's look at the VM, TSO/E, and OS/2 environments and see what is available in each.

20.1   Capturing Responses in VM

In VM, the tools that are available to you are:

- The EXECIO command (with the CP operand) for CP commands
- The DIAG() function for CP commands
- The STACK option for many CMS commands
- The console log (also called spooling the console)

20.1.1   The EXECIO Command (with the CP Operand) for CP Commands

One of the ways a command can be issued to CP is through the EXECIO command. The command is specified on the STRING option, and the output from the command can be directed to the stack or to compound variables (similar to reading files), or the command output can be blocked out completely (this comes in handy when you are writing programs for others to use and you don't want the command output displayed on the screen). Here is an example of issuing a QUERY RDR ALL command:

```
'EXECIO * CP (STRING QUERY RDR ALL'
```

This example will issue the QUERY RDR ALL command, and the return code from the QUERY RDR ALL command, not the one from EXECIO, will be placed in the variable **rc**. The lines will go to the stack, for this is the default way in which EXECIO works. The asterisk in the command tells EXECIO to take *all* the response lines from the command and place them either on the stack or in variables. If a 0 was specified in place of the asterisk, as in

```
'EXECIO 0 CP (STRING QUERY RDR ALL'
```

none of the response lines would be placed on the stack; they would be ignored. They would not go to the screen; they just "go away."

Instead of placing the response lines on the stack or blocking them out, they can be redirected to compound variables by using the STEM option. Consider this next example:

```
'EXECIO * CP (STEM RDR. STRING QUERY RDR ALL'
```

The output from the command, including the header, would be placed in the variables RDR.1, RDR.2, RDR.3, etc. The header would go into RDR.1. The RDR.0 variable would be assigned the number of response lines (one for the header plus one for each file in your reader). If you had sent the lines to the stack and were processing the information in a loop, you would most likely have to issue the PULL instruction to get rid of the header line. Using the technique of the compound variables, you can use the following loop structure:

```
address command
'EXECIO * CP (STEM RDR. STRING QUERY RDR ALL'
if rc = 0
  then
  do i = 2 to rdr.0
    parse var rdr.i originid fileid . . . . . . . fn ft .
    (process the records accordingly)
  end
```

The fact that the loop starts the counter at 2, instead of 1, bypasses (and effectively ignores) the first value, which would be the header.

There is an option that will come in very handy with the EXECIO command when issuing CP commands—the BUFFER option. EXECIO will use an 8K buffer to hold the response lines from CP commands; this represents 101 lines of 80 characters per line of output from the command. If you are issuing a QUERY TIME command, which puts out only 2 lines (and they're not full lines, at that), you are using 8K to hold what is not even 160 bytes. Use the BUFFER option to specify the size of the buffer (take your best guess) that you need for that command. You can specify a value from 0 to 65,535. This represents the number of bytes of output expected.

This is how the EXECIO command can be used to issue CP commands from within your program.

20.1.2 The DIAG() Function for CP Commands

As an alternative to the use of the EXECIO command for issuing commands to CP, the DIAG() function or its cousin, the DIAGRC()

function, can be used.   The DIAG() functions are more efficient than the EXECIO method.   In addition, the size of the buffer that is used to hold the response lines can be changed.   The default size is 4K; that represents 50 lines of a full 80 characters per line of response. You can specify the size of the buffer you need.   Take your best guess; estimate 80 characters per line times the number of lines on your screen times the number of screens worth of response you are expecting.

In contrast to the EXECIO command placing the response lines on the stack or in compound variables, the DIAG() and DIAGRC() functions are just that—functions.   In REXX, a function returns its value(s) to the statement that invoked the function.   The response lines are placed together as one line of data, with a line separator between each line.   The character used for this is '15'x, which can be used in a parsing template to isolate one line from another.

The DIAG() and DIAGRC() functions differ in that the DIAGRC() function will also give you the return code from the CP command; it does this by placing a 16-byte header onto the response line string that is returned by the function.   The form of the response line is as follows:

Bytes   Field
1 – 9   The return code from the CP command.   This value would have gone into the variable RC if the CP command had been issued directly from the program as a host command.
10   A blank to separate the return code from the condition code.
11   The condition code from the CP command.   This is the only way to get this information from a CP command (from a REXX program point of view, that is).
12 – 16   Five blanks to finish off the header on a nice boundary (from a byte/word/doubleword point of view).

Note: There is no '15'x separating the header from the rest of the response line string.

Following the header is the string of response line characters, with a '15'x following each line of response. Here is the code that can be used with the DIAGRC() function:

```
/* for this example, assume about a dozen or so reader files */
qrdr=diagrc(8,'QUERY RDR ALL',1000)
/*  parse out the return code and condition code           */
/*  it's a 16-byte header, so the response lines start at 17 */
parse var qrdr 1 rc . 10 condition_code . 17 qrdr
if rc=0
  then
    do forever
      /*----------------------------------------------------------/
      /-  the template in this example would more likely be  -/
      /-  a bit more elaborate, depending on what the program-/
      /-  is to do with the reposnse lines                  -/
      /----------------------------------------------------------*/
      parse var qrdr line '15'x qrdr
      if qrdr='' then leave

  :

    end
```

If you know what you're looking for, you can treat the response line string as just a string:

```
/*  find the setting for EMSG */
parse value diag(8,'QUERY SET',1000) with 'EMSG' emsgsetting ','
```

20.1.3 The STACK Option for Many CMS Commands

Many of the CMS commands that display information on the screen as the command response can place the response lines on the Program Stack. To accomplish this, these commands will have either a STACK, LIFO, or FIFO option (or some combination thereof). The lines will be placed on the Program Stack, and you can use the PULL (or PARSE PULL) instruction to get the lines into program variables. Here is an example.

```
/*-------------------------------------------------------------/
/- HOWMANY - an exec to display a list of the block sizes   -/
/-          used no a given disk for a given set of files. -/
/- syntax - HOWMANY fn ft fm                                -/
/-          where  fn - the filename (defaults to *)        -/
/-          where  ft - the filetype (defaults to *)        -/
/-          where  fm - the filemode (defaults to A)        -/
/-------------------------------------------------------------*/
arg fn ft fm
/*-------------------------------------------------------------/
/- Let the arguments default if not specified.              -/
/- Initialize the table to 0s.                              -/
/-------------------------------------------------------------*/
fn=word(fn '*',1)
ft=word(ft '*',1)
fm=word(fm 'A',1)
blocklist.=0
/*-------------------------------------------------------------/
/- Issue the host command to get the information...          -/
/- place the response lines on the stack.                   -/
/-------------------------------------------------------------*/
'LISTFILE' fn ft fm' (DATE STACK'
max=0
do queued()
   pull fn ft . . . . blocks .
   max=max(blocks,max)
   blocklist.blocks=blocklist.blocks + 1
   if blocklist.blocks.name=0
     then blocklist.blocks.name= fn
     else blocklist.blocks.name= blocklist.blocks.name fn
end
say "Blocks Used      How Many Files       Which Ones"
say "===========      ==============       =========="
do i = 1 to max
   if blocklist.i > 0
     then say center(i,11)||'        '||center(blocklist.i,14)||,
                          '        '||blocklist.i.name
end
```

Here, the LISTFILE command directs the response lines to the stack. The PULL command is used. Note that there is no PULL statement to get rid of the header line that is displayed on the terminal if this command was issued without the STACK option.

The use of LIFO or FIFO (if available for the given CMS command) determines the order in which the lines are placed on the stack. LIFO (last-in, first-out) is what you can think of as "normal" order. FIFO is "reverse" order.

Note: Some of the CMS commands display a header line of information; some don't display it. Some display it only under certain conditions or options; some display it regardless of the options specified. It is up to the program writer to investigate how each command will work.

20.1.4 The Console Log (Also Called Spooling the Console)

If you need the response from a certain command that does not have an option to stack the response or direct it to compound variables in your program, you can resort to spooling the console. Spooling the console will result in a file being built that captures all the responses that go to the screen when CP is supporting the screen. The use of a full-screen program (XEDIT and ISPF are examples) will cause CP to "give up" control of the screen while that program is running; during that time, responses that go to the screen will not be captured in the console file. Once control returns to CP, the response lines will be placed in the console file. Once you have the information you want, you can issue a command to stop the capturing of the information. The file that was created will now be sent to one of your virtual devices (usually the reader). If the file is directed to your reader, you can receive the file, using the file number (also referred to as the spoolid). The file will then be placed on disk, and you can read it in and retrieve the information you want.

This is not a trivial exercise; it should be used only as a last resort. There are many assumptions that have to be made; for example, does the person running the program have the console spooled already? If so, you can't have two console files at the same time. If you close the console file, it closes it for the user also. This may be a problem. Another point to consider is the receiving of the console file from the reader: to which disk/directory will the file be written? Is there a disk/directory that *can* be written to—does the user running the program have write access/authority? Is there enough space to hold the console log? If not, can sufficient temporary space be obtained?

With the caution stated in the previous paragraph, here is an example of using the console listing to capture a command response:

```
/*-------------------------------------------------------------/
/-  issue the load command and capture the screen response   -/
/-------------------------------------------------------------*/
x=diagrc(8,'SPOOL CONSOLE * START',200)
'LOAD ABC'
x=diagrc(8,'SPOOL CONSOLE CLOSE STOP',200)
parse var x . . . . filenumber .
'SET CMSTYPE HT'
'EXEC RECEIVE' filenumber 'LOAD CONSOLE A3'
'SET CMSTYPE RT'
'EXECIO * DISKR LOAD CONSOLE A (FINIS STEM LOAD.'
&velllip.
```

Of course, capturing the console response means letting the response(s) from the command(s) appear on the screen. This brings up the issue of human factors as it pertains to your program: should your program allow the responses to appear on the screen, or should it "keep things to itself"? This issue is not going to be addressed here;   there are too many "it depends" involved.

20.2 Capturing Responses in TSO/E

In TSO/E, the tool that is available to you is:

- The OUTTRAP() function

20.2.1 The OUTTRAP() Function

The OUTTRAP() function can be used when you write programs that run in the TSO/E address space. It is used before issuing the host command whose response(s) you want to capture. The command response is directed to program variables. The function returns either the string OFF   (if the trapping was turned off) or the name of the variable that is specified to hold the trapped responses.

The command allows you to specify the "base" variable name that will hold the responses, the maximum number of response lines to capture, and whether or not to "overlay" the response variables. Once you specify a "base" variable to hold the output, it will remain in effect until you issue the OUTTRAP() function with the OFF parameter. This will stop the capturing of the command response(s).

The default number of lines that can be trapped is one billion minus 1 (999,999,999). The "base" variable name is appended with a number, thus creating a new variable for each line of response. For example,

```
sendit=outtrap('LISTDS.')
```

will create the variables **listds.1, listds.2, etc.,** up to the number of response lines. The variable **listds.0** will contain the number of response lines that were captured. The variable **listds.trapped** will contain the number of response lines that are available for capturing, from that command. In addition to these variables, the variables **listds.max, listds.0,** and **listds.con** are created. The variable **listds.max** will contain the maximum number of lines that can be captured. This can be changed by specifying a different value as the second parameter to the function. If you do not specify a different maximum, it defaults to 999,999,999 (one short of a billion). If you specify a maximum value that turns out to be less than the number of response from a given command, the **variable.0** will be less than **variable.trapped**.

It is possible to let the command responses from different commands accumulate; this will continue until trapping is turned off or the maximum (either the default or the specified value, whichever comes first) is reached. The last "index value" that was used by a given command is available in the **listds.0** This variable, if it's needed, should be referenced before the next host command is issued. If NOCONCAT is specified, the variables **listds.trapped** and **listds.0** will be equal to each other, assuming that the value specified for the maximum number of lines exceeds the actual number of response lines. The variable **listds.con** contains the string CONCAT or NOCONCAT. If the responses are not concatenated, they will "overlay" the previous set of responses.

It is possible to specify a "base" variable name that has no period(s) in it. For example, specifying the name LISTDS will produce **listds1, listds2, etc.** It is a matter of personal programming style, but the use of the period makes indexing the "response table" much easier for most programs.

To keep your programs clearer and more concise, either use the NOCONCAT parameter with the OUTTRAP() function, or use a different "base" variable name for each host command. This way, there won't be any question as to which range within a given set of variable names contains the information you need from the host command(s).

20.3 Capturing Responses in OS/2

In OS/2, the main tools that are available to you are

- Redirecting the command output to a file

- Piping the command output to another program

20.3.1 Redirecting the Command Output to a File

There are times when you want the output of commands to be redirected to a "place" where your program can get at the information. Sending the command response to a file is one of the ways to achieve this. Once the information is in a file, it can be read in using the LINEIN() function.

To redirect the output from the command, issue the command with the '>' symbol, followed by a name of a file. For example,

```
'DIR *.CMD > EXECLIST'
```

will take the output from the DIR command and place the line in a file called EXECLIST. All this takes place within the current directory. Information on files from other (sub)directories can be obtained by using the backslash and perhaps even a different disk letter.

If you make use of the same file a second (or later) time, as in

```
'DIR A:*.CMD > EXECLIST'
```

the file EXECLIST will be overwritten. If you want to have the information from both commands in the same file, double the '>' symbol. This way,

```
'DIR C:*.CMD >> EXECLIST'
'DIR B:*.CMD >> EXECLIST'
'DIR A:*.CMD >> EXECLIST'
```

will produce the list of .CMD files in the root directory for the three disks in the file EXECLIST. EXECLIST is located on the "active" disk.

One thing to keep in mind when issuing commands, and capturing the responses, is header information and separator lines are included in the file.

20.3.2 Piping the Command Output to Another Program

In addition to redirecting the output from a command to a file, you can make use of something called "piping." This involves the use of the split vertical bar (on some keyboards, there are two vertical bar keys, one solid, one split; if you have the choice, use the split vertical one). It is similar to redirecting the output to a file, but there is no "file" that is used as the intermediate step. The output from the command is fed directly to the second command you list; for example,

```
'DIR | RXQUEUE'
```

will take the output from the command and place it on the stack. The PULL instruction can then be used to get the lines into the program. This method does not use a file as an intermediary. Of course, you would have to reissue the command if you wanted to get at the output response more than once—the decision between using a file to hold the information and piping it to another command/program is up to you. There are valid arguments to be made on both sides.

Chapter 21.
Can I Make a REXX
"Include" File?

21.1 What Is an "Include" File?

An "include" file is a section of code that is common to many
programs. It resides physically separate from these programs, and
becomes part of the programs when each one is run. It differs
from an external piece of code in that it does not have its own set
of variables; instead, it becomes part of the program that is
"including" it (as if it were part of the program all along).

As an example, consider the set of programs that involve
themselves with production of the widget. There could be a
common set of data values that represent the manufacturing
specifications of the widget. For instance, the list of materials
that make up the widget, the profit margin for each version of the
widget that is produced, the cost of each material part, the
number of people involved with each stage of the manufacturing
process, etc.—all of these data values can be considered vital to
different programs that focus on different aspects of the widget
manufacturing process. There may be one program that is
responsible for producing the inventory orders. Another may be
concerned with the scheduling of manufacturing personnel. Yet

215

another may be involved with cost accounting for the overall project. Each of these programs needs some of the information described here.

If there was some change in the technology that directly affected the method of manufacturing the widget, or if it affected the cost of the material parts that constitute the widget, then each program would have to be modified to reflect the new "vital stats" of the widget. The possibility of one (or some) of the programs not being updated correctly (if at all) would exist.

There may be simply a collection of assignment statements in the include file, or there may be some additional instructions that add some logic to the program. When you decide to create an include file, keep in mind that this code can be used by more than one program; limit the code placed in the include file to that code which should/must be common to the programs.

If there were some way to keep all that code together, and just change it in one place, the maintenance of the software would be facilitated. REXX provides some tools to assist in this endeavor.

21.2 How Can REXX Help Me?

The "tools" that will help you in this effort are the INTERPRET instruction and the I/O mechanism (the EXECIO command or the LINEIN() function, depending on the environment in which the program will run). These tools, when used with a set of compound variables, provide the mechanism for a REXX include file.

Here is the recipe:

1. Load the statements into compound variables.

2. Loop through the compound variables, and interpret them.

21.2.1 Load the Statements into Compound Variables

The use of the compound variable to create a table (or array, vector, matrix, or linked list, if you prefer) is recommended because of the way it can be processed using a loop structure. Given this usage of a table, a simple numeric index should suffice. Any relatively complex table structure can be in the statements themselves, and need not be a major concern of the compound variables, which will simply serve as the temporary storage area, so to speak, for the include file statements. Once the interpreting of these include file statements is complete, the table that was used to hold them can be DROPped, thus logically (and, at least, in the case of CMS, physically) freeing up the table to be used for other purposes.

If, for example, the first three statements in the include file were

```
number.of.parts=7
number.of.build.steps=10
number.of.assemblers=3
```

there would be a need for a way to execute these statements inside the "original" program (the one that wants to include them). Again, if this file were executed as an external piece of code, the variables inside the include file would be "local" and the program that did the calling would not be able to take advantage of the values set up in the external file. The placing of the statements into compound variables in the original program, and the subsequent interpreting of the new compound variables, is what makes these variables known to the program that is "doing the including."

Let's look at both tools that can be used for this. The EXECIO command will come into play in the CMS, and TSO/E environments. The LINEIN() function will come into play in the OS/2 and OS/400 environments.

21.2.1.1 The EXECIO command

The command option you want to use here is the STEM option. It takes the blank-delimited string that follows, and creates a table of compound variables with that string as the stem. When specifying the stem, make sure to use upper-case characters. This will avoid any problems with the way the REXX variables are stored and accessed. You do not have to use a period in the string that follows the STEM option. If you had specified STEM X, the variables created would be **X1, X2, X3, etc.** Specifying the period, as in STEM X., will produce the variables **X.1, X.2, X.3, etc.** In both cases, the **X.0** (or **X0**) variable will contain the number of variables created. Thus,

```
'EXECIO * DISKR 'infile' (FINIS STEM INCLUDE.'
```

would create the table INCLUDE., and INCLUDE.0 would contain
the number of entries in the table. This variable can then be used
in the following loop:

```
do i = 1 to include.0
   interpret include.i
end
drop include.
```

Keep in mind that the INTERPRET instruction is a "two-step"
instruction. The first step is to create a statement by evaluating
variables (in this case, the variables starting with include.) and
concatenating them with literal strings (there are none in this
case). The second step is to execute the newly created statement,
as if it had been written into the program originally. This is how
the external file can contain assignment (or other) statements that
become part of the file that is "including" it. The variables
referenced in the include file are now part of the program, and
their values can be used at will.

Once the include file is interpreted, there is no need for the
table that contained the statements. DROPping the stem of the
table will restore the table variables to their uninitialized state,
thus allowing the reuse of the variables without concern about
their previous values.

21.2.1.2 The LINEIN() function

The LINEIN() function does not have the STEM option that the
EXECIO command has; it has to be used a bit differently.
Borrowing from the earlier example of using the LINEIN function
in a loop, we now have

```
do i=1
   if lines(infile) = 0 then leave
   include.i=linein(infile)
   include.0=i
end
```

The LINEIN() function, treating the file as an input stream, will
read in one line at a time. The loop structure can vary, but the
effect is to build the table in its entirety first. Following that, the
following code can be used:

```
do i = 1 to include.0
   interpret include.i
end
drop include.
```

Keep in mind that the INTERPRET instruction is a "two-step" instruction. The first step is to create a statement by evaluating variables (in this case, the variables starting with include.) and concatenating them with literal strings (there are none in this case). The second step is to execute the newly created statement, as if it had been written into the program originally. This is how the external file can contain assignment (or other) statements that become part of the file that is "including" it. The variables referenced in the include file are now part of the program, and their values can be used at will.

Once the include file is interpreted, there is no need for the table that contained the statements. DROPping the stem of the table will restore the table variables to their uninitialized state, thus allowing the reuse of the variables without concern about their previous values.

21.2.2 Chapter Summary

There are several different ways in which each of these examples could have been coded. In keeping with the initial thrust of this book, these examples are provided to give you one way of using the REXX language to accomplish these tasks. The different environments in which the REXX language can be used (mainframe, personal computer) offer exciting contrasts in some areas of the implementations of REXX. The similarities are equally exciting. With this chapter, you have reached the end of the book. It is yet another tool that will help you understand the world of REXX.

Glossary

Abuttal concatenation. The process of combining two terms in a REXX statement, where the terms may be either numeric strings or nonnumeric strings, depending on the form of abuttal concatenation used. For example, specifying a variable name right next to a character string will result in the two terms being combined without a blank space between them. This works only for character string to variable (the order of which is not important). When using this form of abuttal concatenation, watch out for the use of the variable x, which could cause your character string to be interpreted as a hexadecimal number!

The second form of abuttal concatenation involves the use of the || character (requires two keystrokes). This form will allow the abuttal of anything to anything (variables to variables, strings to strings). This form also results in the terms being concatenated with no blank space between.

ARG instruction. The instruction used inside REXX programs to access the input argument string to a program when used in the "main section" of the program (see Main section), and to access the routine input argument string when used in an internal routine (subroutine or function).

The ARG instruction accesses the input argument string and places the values supplied in the variables listed on the template (see Templates).

Arguments at the start of the program. Those arguments supplied in the input argument string to the program. These values are accessed when the ARG instruction is used in the program's main section.

Arguments in REXX. The values supplied as part of the input argument string either to the program itself or to a routine inside the program (the routine could be inside the program itself, or it could be external to the program).

Arithmetic operators. The operators that REXX uses when performing arithmetic. They are + (addition), - (subtraction), * (multiplication), / (division), ** (exponentiation), // (integer division), % (remainder division). These operators are dyadic; that is, they take an operand on each side. The parentheses (),, while not true arithmetic operators, can be used to group arithmetic operations together, according to arithmetic rules.

Arrays in REXX. Compound variables. See definition of compound variables for more information.

Blackhole. A period (.) used in a template on a PARSE instruction. Used to selectively ignore values that would have been picked up had a variable been placed in that spot on the template. Values picked up by a blackhole are "discarded."

Blank concatenation. The process of combining pieces of a program statement in REXX. Blank concatenation is more prevalent than might appear to the casual observer. An example of this is the fact that x = 3 and x = 3 and x   =   3 are functionally equivalent. When blank concatenation is used, the first blank is kept, and the others are "discarded" or ignored.

Box comment. A single comment that spans more than one line and uses characters to make a "border" for readability purposes, or a collection of many single-line comments, with the top and bottom comments using some "border" characters. Usually contains helpful information that describes some part of the program.

Capturing command responses. The process by which responses from host commands are "redirected" from the display to storage inside the realm of the program, by sending them either to the Program Stack (data queue), or to program variables.

Capturing host commands. See Capturing command responses.

Case. The set of alphabetic characters used to create the REXX program; usually referred to as UPPER, lower, or mIxEd.

Catenation. See concatenation.

CENTER() routine. One of the REXX built-in routines. Used to center characters within a user-specified field length. Listed in the manual as a function, but can be accessed by the CALL command as if it were a "built-in subroutine."

CENTRE() function. See CENTER() routine.

Character output. The writing to a file of one character at a time, as opposed to one line at a time.

Character string. A set of characters used in a REXX instruction or a host command that is surrounded by a set of single or double quotes. There can be several character strings in the same statement in the program. The maximum length of a character string depends on the environment in which REXX is running (for example, REXX in the VM environment allows a maximum length of 250 characters).

CHARIN() function. The function used in REXX in the OS/2 environment to read data in one character at a time. The character read is returned as a function value, similar to the way other functions work. CHARIN can also be used with the CALL instruction, and the character returned would be available to the program in the variable RESULT.

CHAROUT() function. The function used in REXX in the OS/2 environment to write data out one character at a time. The character written is supplied as an input parameter to the function. CHAROUT can also be used with the CALL instruction, and the character written would be supplied as a parameter on the CALL statement itself.

CHARS() function. The function used in REXX in the OS/2 environment to tell whether any more characters exist in the stream (file) or not. Useful as the method for determining end-of-file when reading character by character. Returns a 1 if more exist; 0 if no more exist.

Coding guidelines. A collection of statements that can be used to help guide one through the program development process, focusing mainly on the method of physically writing the program statements. The concept of program readability comes into play here in a very strong way. The underlying idea of the techniques suggested in this book is the premise that a program that is easier to read will be easier to understand, and thus easier to maintain.

Coding techniques. See Coding guidelines.

Combining program statements. Placing more than one statement on a line in a REXX program. This is accomplished by using a semicolon (;) as the statement separator. Be careful not to confuse this with the use of the semicolon as a clause separator; just because a semicolon is present does not necessarily mean that it signifies the start of a new statement. Thus, you have to be careful when using semicolons.

If you are placing two or more statements on the same physical line of the program, you need to put a semicolon between each of the statements.

Command output. The lines of response that typically go to the display device when the command is issued outside of a REXX program.

Command responses. See Command output.

Commands. Those statements that are not part of the REXX instruction set, but belong to the environment in which the REXX program is running. For example, the commands could belong to ISPF, CMS, OS/2, TSO, etc.

Commas in REXX. See Line continuation.

Comments. The characters /* and */, and any characters that are placed between these character sets. REXX will not process any of the statements between the /* and the */, but it will look to see if any other sets of these characters are contained therein, thus allowing for the "nesting" of comments.

Compound variables. Variables that have a multi-part name. Used to simulate arrays, matrices, tables, or vectors. The parts of the variable name are separated by a period. The variable name must follow the rules for variable names, in that it can not start with a number or a period. The first part of the variable name (up to and including the first period) is called the *stem*. The stem can be thought of as the "name" of the table. The remaining parts of the compound variable name will be evaluated and contacenated, with the resulting string being the actual variable name under which a value will be set/fetched.

Concatenation. The process of combining numeric strings with nonnumeric strings in a statement in a REXX program. This can be accomplished by abuttal concatenation or by blank concatenation (both of these are defined in this glossary).

Continuing lines. See Line continuation.

COPIES() function. One of the built-in routines provided as part of the REXX language. These routines may be invoked as functions or CALLed as subroutines. The COPIES() function returns a string of n copies of a user-specified string.

Default values (for arguments/parameters). The values that get used when no input parameter is supplied by the user (or the calling routine). They answer the question "What will I use as a value if no one gives me a value to use?"

Double quotes. The " character (only one keystroke for this character).

Editor macros in REXX. Programs which issue commands to an editor. These commands can be used to alter the appearance of the file on the screen, process the data in the file, or both.

EXEC. A file in VM that contains program statements written in REXX. The program statements can be written in CMS EXEC or EXEC 2, but this book is about REXX.

EXECIO. The host command used in the CMS and TSO environments to perform input and output operations to files. In CMS, can also be used to issue host commands to CP.

EXPOSE instruction. An instruction used in conjunction with the PROCEDURE instruction to allow a mix of global and local variables. Variables are separated by one or more blanks. Used in internal routines (subroutines or functions). See also Global variables and Local variables

EXPOSE statement. See EXPOSE instruction.

External subprograms. Pieces of code which are not part of the calling program, but can be CALLed or invoked as a function (using the parentheses). Can be written in Assembler and other languages, but if written in an EXEC language, are to be written in REXX.

File I/O. Reading and writing files and/or datasets.

File naming in CMS. The name of a CMS file has three parts: The filename, the filetype, and the filemode. These parts are separated by a blank. See the later descriptions for these parts.

File naming in OS/2. The name of a file in OS/2 has two parts, the name and the extension, which are separated by a period (.). In addition, the file can have a path designation, which identifies the (sub)directory in which the file resides. The extension of the file is optional, and is three characters maximum in length.

File naming in TSO. The name of a *basic* file in TSO has up to four parts, depending on whether it is a sequential data set, or a member of a partitioned data set (PDS). If it is a sequential data set, it can have up to three parts, separated by periods. If it is a member of a PDS, it can have up to four names, with the fourth being a name in parentheses.

Fileid. In CMS, the filename, filetype, and filemode. In TSO, the project, group, type, and optionally the member. In OS/2, the name and the extension; the path is optional and precedes the fileid.

Filemode. The third part of a fileid in CMS. Consists of a letter which identifies the disk or directory on which the file resides and a number (0 to 6) which defines some of the file's attributes (i.e., temporary file, private file, etc.).

Filename. The first part of a fileid in CMS. Consists of up to eight characters.

Filetype. The second part of a fileid in CMS. Consists of up to eight characters.

Filing programs. The process of saving a copy of a program to a disk or directory or library.

FIND function. One of the built-in routines supplied as part of the REXX language. The FIND function identifies the position of a blank-delimited string in another string.

FINIS. In CMS, the command used to close a file that was opened. Can be specified as an option to the EXECIO instruction, or can be issued as a host command.

Floating-point numbers. Scientific notation, e.g., 2E + 10.

FORMAT() function. One of the built-in routines supplied as part of the REXX language. The format function rounds and formats numbers.

Formatting output. The process of "lining" output in columns or spacing terms in a certain way to improve readability of the output.

Functions. Routines that are invoked by specifying the name followed by a set of parentheses.

Global variable. A variable that can be accessed or modified from any part of a REXX program. In REXX, global variables are the default. You have to use the PROCEDURE instruction to get local variables.

Grids in REXX. Compound variables. See definition of compound variables for more information.

Host commands. Commands that do not belong to the set of REXX instructions. They are evaluated by REXX, and then "passed" over to the host environment. For example, they can be TSO or OS/2 or CMS or CP or ISPF (etc.) commands that are issued from within a REXX program.

IF instruction. One of the REXX instructions that provide program logic direction.

IF-THEN-ELSE. One of the REXX instructions that provide program logic direction.

Ignoring a parameter. The use of a blackhole in a template or the use of commas in a template to cause parameters to be "shifted" one way or another, so that they will not be picked up in variables.

In-line comments. Comments that occupy the same physical line as program code. Not recommended by this author, because they can cause a problem during program maintenance.

Include files in REXX. Files that are external to the REXX program and contain REXX statements. Generally, these files are read in, and interpreted using the INTERPRET instruction.

Include macros in REXX. See Include files in REXX.

Indentation. The process of adding additional blanks on a line of code to show the level of "logic subordination" as it relates to the lines that precede it.

INDEX function. One of the REXX built-in routines supplied as part of the REXX language. The INDEX function returns the starting position of a string in another.

Inline comments. See In-line comments.

Input arguments. Values that are supplied to a program or routine.

Input parameters. Values that are supplied to a program or routine.

Input/output. See File I/O.

INSERT() function. One of the built-in routines supplied as part of the REXX language. The INSERT function is used to insert a character string into another, at a user-specified starting position.

Internal subprograms. Sections of a REXX program delimited by a label and a RETURN instruction. Can be accessed as either a subroutine or a function.

INTERPRET instruction. One of the REXX instructions. Allows for the dynamic creation of a statement (REXX instruction or host command) within a REXX program.

JUSTIFY() function. One of the built-in routines supplied as part of the REXX language. The justify function is used to right- and left-justify text within a specified field width.

Leading characters. Those characters that are on the "front end" of a string. Usually used in context of the STRIP() function.

LEFT() function. One of the built-in routines supplied as part of the REXX language. The left function is used to left-justify text within a specified field width. If the string is longer than the specified field width, the "left-hand" portion of the string is returned.

Levels of quotes. The use of both single and double quotes in a program statement. When looked at in the same way as parentheses are used, one set of quotes is removed from the program statement. When looked at as REXX looks at the statement, the first quote encountered (single or double) becomes the "quotes" for that string. If the other type of quote is encountered, it is looked at as simply another character; thus it is left in the string, giving the impression that one level of quotes has been removed from the string.

Line continuation. The process of physically separating part of a program statement across a line-end boundary. This is typically done to improve the readability of a program statement in that it allows the entire statement to be read without having to scroll left or right to see the entire statement.

LINEIN() function. The function used to read in a "stream" of data to a REXX program. The LINEIN() function reads in one line at a time from the input stream (in many cases a file).

LINEOUT() function. The function used to write out a "stream" of data from a REXX program. The LINEOUT() function writes out one line at a time to the output stream (in many cases a file).

Literals. Characters contained inside a pair of quotes. Can show up in any of several statements in a REXX program.

Literals in parsing. Character strings enclosed in quotes that are used as "pattern matching" strings or "synchronization characters." They are used to "line things up" so that the parsing into template variables occurs as expected.

Loading programs into storage. In a VM environment, the process of using the EXECLOAD command to bring REXX programs into virtual storage. In a TSO environment, the process of loading REXX programs into VLF (Virtual Lookaside Facility) controlled storage. The benefit of loading REXX programs into storage is the reduced disk I/O when the external pieces of code are "called." The disadvantage of this practice is the use of more storage while the program is running, as opposed to using the storage as each piece of external code is brought in and out of storage.

Local variables. Variables that exist in a routine or function that uses the PROCEDURE instruction. The "caller's" variables are not known to the routine, and any variables that are set up within that routine are not known to the caller. In addition, the variables that get created within the routine are "gone" after the routine ends. The "knowing or not" of variables is determined by each routine that is referenced in a program. The default is to have global variables (those that are accessible throughout the program).

Lower case. The use of lower-case letters when coding a REXX program.

Macros in REXX (include files). See Include files in REXX for more information.

Main section. The logical "first" part of a program; usually found before internal routines (subroutines or functions).

Matrices in REXX. Compound variables. See definition of compound variables for more information.

Mixed case. Combining lower- and upper-case letters in coding a REXX program.

Modularity. The use of internal/external routines in a program to separate "logical" units of the program.

Multiple comments. The use of many single-line comments on consecutive lines, with common starting and ending column positions, thus giving the impression of a comment "box." Also, a single comment that spans more than one line in a program, using "border" characters to give the impression of a comment "box."

One-line program. A program written in a purely horizontal fashion, occupying only one physical line in a file. Necessitates extensive use of the semicolon.

Operators. The collection of characters that allow arithmetic and logic expressions in a REXX program.

OVERLAY() function. One of the built-in routines supplied as part of the REXX language. The OVERLAY() function is used to replace characters in a string with other characters.

Pad character. A user-specified character that is used when a requested string length is too long. In many cases, the default pad character is a blank (' ').

Parameters in REXX. The values supplied as part of the input argument string either to the program itself, or to a routine inside the program (the routine could be inside the program itself, or it could be external to the program).

Parentheses in the template. Parentheses are used in a template to identify variables that contain control information to direct the parsing of a string into variables contained in the template.

PARSE instruction. The REXX instruction used to perform parsing of character strings. See Parsing for more information.

Parsing. The process of splitting up a string, and taking parts of that string and storing them into variables. A template is used that contains the variables that will receive the values. In addition, the template can contain control information to direct the parsing.

Piping command output. The process of taking command output that would normally go to a display, and passing it into another program as input. The concept of piping can be seen in OS/2 and CMS environments.

POS() function. One of the built-in routines supplied as part of the REXX language. The POS() function is used to return the starting position of a string within another.

Preloading program into storage. See Loading programs into storage.

PROCEDURE instruction. The REXX instruction that is used to provide "local variables" in a routine (and those called from within). With local variables, any variables that existed previously are not known, nor will any variables that are created in the routine be known once the routine ends.

Program. A physical collection of instructions that will be translated to a form that the computer can work with; usually contained in a file. The programs in this book are written in the REXX (REstructured, eXtended eXecutor) language.

Program format. The general view of a program from a readability perspective. Includes the concept of internal and external routines to provide modularity of the program code, as well as topics such as use of mixed case for program statements, etc.

Program stack. In CMS, the system-provided data queue. See System-provided data queue for more information.

Program structure. The general view of a program from a readability perspective. Includes the concept of internal and external routines to provide modularity of the program code, as well as topics such as use of mixed case for program statements, etc.

PULL instruction. The REXX instruction used to read one line from the system-provided data queue or from the display (if the data queue is empty). Uses a template to store the values retrieved.

QUEUE instruction. The REXX instruction that is used to place a line of information/data on the system-provided data queue. The information is placed at the logical bottom end of the queue (also called FIFO, first-in first-out). Specifying the QUEUE instruction without any data will cause a null entry to be place on the queue.

Quotes. See Single quote and Double quotes.

Redirecting command output. The taking of command responses that would normally go to the display, and causing them to go to another destination (a file or some program variables, for instance).

REVERSE() function. One of the built-in routines supplied as part of the REXX language. The reverse function is used to reverse a character string and return the reversed form of the string.

REXX. The REstructured eXtended eXecutor language.

RIGHT() function. One of the built-in routines supplied as part of the REXX language. The RIGHT() function is used to right-justify text within a specified field width. If the string is longer than the specified field width, the "right-hand" portion of the string is returned.

Routines. Internal subprograms in a REXX program that are accessed via the CALL instruction. When accessed in this way, the values returned are placed in a variable called RESULT. By default, all variables are known throughout the program (in other words, they are global). This can be controlled by the use of the PROCEDURE and EXPOSE instructions.

Saving programs. The process of SAVEing or FILEing programs to secondary storage devices.

SAY instruction. The REXX instruction that displays information and text on the console. Each SAY generates a new line on the console, but each SAY can display more characters than the screen width. In this case, the line of text will "wrap around" to the next line. The SAY instruction evaluates an expression, and thus can perform arithmetic, function calls, etc.

Scientific notation. One of the ways in which numbers in REXX can be presented. 1.5E + 04 is an example of scientific notation. The exponent part is expressed in base 10.

Scope of variables. The extent to which variables are available for access, usually expressed in terms of main program and subroutine sections. See also Global variable. By default, the scope of program variables is the entire program. This can be modified by using the PROCEDURE and EXPOSE instructions.

SELECT instruction. One of the REXX instructions that allows decisions to be programmed into the program logic. The SELECT should be thought of as "a bunch of IF statements that have a common ELSE" instead of as a CASE statement. The major difference here is that most implementions of a CASE statement limit the programmer to checking only one variable for many values. While this can also be accomplished by SELECT, the WHEN clauses (which are the parts that "ask the questions") can be used to check *any* variables (or combination of variables and functions). This capability provides for more complex logic to be programmed using SELECT.

Semicolons. Used to separate clauses in a REXX program statement. In addition, the semicolon is used when two or more statements are to be placed on the same physical line in the program file. With the exception of the case in which two or more statements are to be on the same line in the program file, the semicolon is not required by syntax. One additional exception to this is the IF statement; if an entire IF-THEN-ELSE structure is to be on one line in the file, there must be a semicolon before the ELSE.

Separating instructions. The use of semicolons. See Semicolons for more information.

Single comment. The characters /* and */ (respectively, the start and end of a comment) and any characters that are between. Comments in REXX are "skipped over" (that is, they are nonexecutable statements).

Single quote. The character ' that is used to start literal strings in a REXX program statement. Identifies nonvariable terms. Usually used in pairs.

SPACE() function. One of the built-in routines supplied as part of the REXX language. The SPACE() function is used to realign blank-delimited character strings with a user-specified number of spaces between the strings. The number can be 0 or greater.

Storing programs. The process of saving programs to secondary storage devices. This is accomplished by using instructions such as SAVE and FILE.

STRIP() function. One of the built-in routines supplied as part of the REXX language. The STRIP() function is used to remove leading, trailing, or both leading and trailing characters from a string.

Subprograms. Internal routines in a REXX program that are accessed via the CALL instruction. When accessed in this way, the values returned are placed in a variable called RESULT. By default, all variables are known throughout the program (in other words, they are global). This can be controlled by the use of the PROCEDURE and EXPOSE instructions.

Subroutines. Internal subprograms in a REXX program that are accessed via the CALL instruction. When accessed in this way, the values returned are placed in a variable called RESULT. By default, all variables are known throughout the program (in other words, they are global). This can be controlled by the use of the PROCEDURE and EXPOSE instructions.

Synchronization strings. See definition of Literal strings. Used in a template in PARSE, ARG, and PULL instructions.

System-provided data queue. A temporary storage area that is available to a REXX program for storing of data/information for use by a later part of the same program, or for an external program. Can be "divided" to allow a degree of integrity between the lines of data that are stored therein.

Tables in REXX. Compound variables. See Compound variables for more information.

Templates. The list of variables and other control characters that are used with the PARSE, ARG, and PULL instructions. The variables listed on the template get modified by the parsing action, and are filled in with some value. In some cases, it is possible that the "value" that gets used to set one or more of the variables is the null string, identified by two quotes next to each other without a blank in between.

Templates using numbers. The numbers that are used to direct the parsing action. The numbers can be absolute or relative. If absolute, they identify the character column position. If relative, they reposition the "character pointer" by saying "go ahead" or "go back" so many characters.

Templates using variables. The list of variables used in a PARSE instruction (also in ARG and PULL). Each variable that is listed on a template will be filled in with some value. That value may be data or may be the null string (''). The variables on the template are filled in "left to right."

Trailing characters. Those characters that are on the "back end" of a string. Usually used in a context of the STRIP() function.

TRUNC() function. One of the built-in routines supplied as part of the REXX language. The TRUNC() function is used to truncate a character string at a given point.

Truncating numbers. The process of using the TRUNC() function to truncate (not round) a number.

Upper case. The characters A through Z. When dealing with host commands, it is prudent to place the nonvariable portions of the statements in upper-case—the alphabetic characters, that is.

Variables.   The set of symbolic names used in a REXX program to refer to storage locations for program information and data.

Vectors in REXX.   Compound variables.   See definition of compound variables for more information.

WORDPOS() function.   One of the built-in routines supplied as part of the REXX language.   The WORDPOS() function is used to identify the ordinal position of a blank-delimited string within another string.

ZONE.   The set of columns that will be used to control a search operation (for example, the EXECIO command or the XEDIT LOCATE command).

Index

X